THEY SAID
IT WOULD BE FUN

A Hilarious Journey Learning
to Hike the NH 48

KENNETH BOSSE

About the cover:

This is a picture of my first hike in winter conditions. It just happened to be Mt. Monroe, which is one of the Presidentials.

The gentleman standing tall on the left is David Salois, at that time the Chief of Police for Raymond, NH. Dave is a phenomenal athlete and also part Micmac Indian. I'm the other guy. I call this pic, "Micmac and Big Mack". You probably can't see it, but I'm actually trying to put my lungs back into my body.

ISBN: 978-1-7343315-0-9

DEDICATION

I dedicate this book to all the men and women of New Hampshire Search and Rescue.

When someone is in trouble in the New Hampshire woods, the first responders are a group of specially trained officers of the New Hampshire Fish and Game Department. These officers coordinate all rescues and facilitate other specialized Search and Rescue teams within the State who are trained in winter, rapid-water or cliff rescues. These men and women respond no matter what Mother Nature is dispensing, often times at risk to their own lives.

With the explosive growth of adventurers wandering into the New Hampshire mountains, these Search and Rescue teams are responding to more calls than ever.

The profits of this book are a way of supporting NH SAR and saying, "Thank you." It's comforting to know the best of the best are always ready.

CAST OF CHARACTERS

No names have been changed to protect the innocent because no one is innocent in this group.

Ian Kenney: At 28, Ian is the youngest. He saw some of my Facebook posts and wanted to give a 4,000 footer a try. He was hooked immediately. He's a great guy and makes a nice addition to the crew.

Dave Salois: At the time Dave was Chief of Police for Raymond, NH. A runner, cyclist and avid hiker, he was the one that pointed me to the NH Whites. He is also the main instigator in the group - always starting stuff despite his innocent expression. Dave is 50 and a super nice guy.

Keith Tilton: Nickname - The Old Fella. He's 70, a jogger and a good friend. Keith went along on these hikes to keep me from dying alone.

Ian, Dave and Keith are great guys individually, but together they created a foul chemistry. The abuse I took was horrible. And I never (hardly) did anything to deserve it!

Ian, Dave & Keith

INTRODUCTION

To receive the patch from the Appalachian Mountain Club (AMC) for the completion of hiking all forty-eight 4,000 footers in New Hampshire, you must record the dates and jot down a few notes about each one. There is no time limit for completion. Some of the stories included in this book tell of a few mountains I had climbed earlier in my life and have no desire to ever set foot on again. One of my later hiking companions, David, climbs these mountains again and again because… well quite frankly, he's a lunatic! Not me! I am a one-and-done kinda guy. I only want the patch because there's just something about putting your body through a living hell forty-eight times for the bragging rights of a $4 patch.

CONTENTS

Acknowledgments   i

Author's Note   ii

How This All Began   iii

1   The Story of Mt. Washington   1

2   The Story of Mt. Lafayette & Mt. Lincoln   5

3   The Story of Mt. Cannon   7

4   The Story of Mt. Waumbek   11

5   The Story of Mt. Jackson   17

6   The Story of Mt. Tecumseh   23

7   The Story of Mt. Hale   27

8   The Story of Mt. Pierce & Mt. Eisenhower   33

9   The Story of Mt. Willey, Mt. Field & Mt. Tom   39

10   The Story of Mt. Garfield   45

11   The Pawtuckaway Loop   51

12   The Story of Mt. Monroe   57

13   The Story of Mt. Osceola   63

14   The Story of Mt. Liberty   67

15   The Story of Mt. Passaconaway   73

16   The Story of Mt. Roberts   77

17   The Story of Mt. Cabot   81

18   The Story of Mt. Flume, Part 1   89

19   The Story of Mt. Osceola & East Peak   93

20	The Story of Mt. Flume… Again	99
21	The Story of Mt. Isolation	103
22	The Story of Mt. Whiteface	109
23	The Story of Mt. Moriah	115
24	The Story of the Tripyramids	121
25	The Story of North & South Kinsman	127
26	The Story of North & South Twin Mountains	131
27	The Story of the Bonds	135
28	The Story of Mt. Carrigain	141
29	The Story of Mt. Zealand	151
30	The Story of Mt. Hancock & South Hancock	155
31	The Story of Mt. Carter Dome	161
32	The Story of Middle Carter	167
33	The Story of Mt. Galehead	173
34	The Story of South Carter	177
35	The Story of the Wildcats	181
36	The Story of Mt. Adams & Mt. Madison	187
37	The Story of Mt. Moosilauke	193
38	The Story of Mt. Owl's Head	197
39	The Story of Mt. Jefferson, Sweet #48	203
40	Cannon Mountain, Part 2	209
41	Friends	215

ACKNOWLEDGMENTS

To my loving wife Darlene, who always encouraged me
to hike higher and higher… as she took out
more and more life insurance on me.

To all my friends who encouraged me to put my short stories into
a book and then would not buy it. I can never say thank you
enough – because once would be way too much.

Much thanks to my faithful hiking buddies. Who else would be so
quick to take pictures as my life was in peril?

Also, many thanks to Kathleen Cole, a life-long friend
who did the editing. Kathleen, a schoolteacher for 40 years,
graciously responded to my plea for help; she edited all the
punctuation and speeling. (Ha, gotcha!)

Authors Note:

How do you write 48 different stories about 48 similar hikes?
Well, you can't. These stories have a lot in common.
Namely, I struggled and suffered on every single one.
I would love to report that they had gotten easier but alas, NO!
I hiked over 98 mountains in 2 1/2 years and it still hurts when I hike.
Now I find I can't stop. It's a disease.

Here is something to take into consideration:
This book is not meant to be educational, it's funny.
"Laughter does good like a medicine."

My recommendation is to read two or so chapters a day.
This will give you many days of humor.

Laugh with me, laugh at me... I don't care. Just laugh.

HOW THIS ALL BEGAN

In the summer of 1972, the movie *Jeremiah Johnson*, starring Robert Redford, hit the theaters. I was an impressionable fourteen-year-old and a movie about a true-blue mountain man was more than my hormones could handle. The tough winter conditions, Indians, bears, etc., were almost too much. I discovered my calling and was destined to become a mountain man. That next winter, wearing old-fashioned wooden snowshoes and with a 22-caliber handgun strapped to my side, I started exploring the wonders of the woods behind my house. However, it would not be until two years later when I got my driver's license that I would have the freedom to venture into the mountains of NH.

I didn't know what I didn't know. That's to say I was a train wreck waiting to happen. A map showed Mt. Chocorua, a 3,497 foot beauty that was the most southerly and shortest drive on my northward trek. I had an aluminum external frame backpack that I loaded with a sleeping bag, tent, stove, six-pack of Coke, two cans of Boston Baked Beans, three cans of Vienna Sausage, (yes, I know what they're made of and I still think they're delicious) and about 30 pounds of other stuff a mountain man would need for an overnighter. The pack probably weighed in the ballpark of a freight train. My dreamy imagination envisioned myself at the top of the mountain, by a small pond, on a nice patch of grass, tent pitched westward facing the fading sunshine, sitting by my stove eating dinner, keeping my eyes peeled for Indians.

Reality was a quickly advancing storm. I arrived at the Piper Trail head around 9 a.m. on a hot, humid August Saturday. The first pin to deflate my balloon was how many other hikers were there and not one of them was an Indian. I put on my pack, which almost pulled me over backward, and with youthful enthusiasm headed up the trail. Birds chirping, sun shining, it was euphoria. I figured I'd hike about a mile up a moderate grade and arrive at a grass-laden summit. Instead, I found myself struggling up a trail so steep that I was panting like a dog with asthma. The higher I went, the hotter it got. I think the forecast that day called for temps that would allow cooking an egg on the hood of your car. At one point I almost fainted when I experienced tunnel vision, ringing in my ears and a spinning sensation like a top. It was exactly the same sensation I had as a kid when I heard my teachers ask for my book reports. I grabbed a small tree and hung on for dear life. Just then some hikers passed me and commented, "That pack doesn't look like fun." How perceptive! I dug deep within, pushed on and summited after a hand-over-hand rock scramble near the top. There was no pond other than the sweat that was puddling under my feet. There was no flat grass area. In fact, there wasn't even a flat area big enough to put my two feet side by side. This mountain peak was like a granite pyramid. I looked around, took some quick mental notes on NH mountains, deleted my dreams of becoming a mountain man, and headed down the trail to the nearest ice cream stand. I drove home having never even opened my backpack. The agony of defeat! It would be three years before I returned to attempt another mountain hike and that was only because I was using drugs.

But the forty-eight? That was to come later…

Here is what I can remember about some of the earlier experiences in the New Hampshire hills.

1 FIRST, THE STORY OF
MOUNT WASHINGTON

Yup, the big one, "THE ROCKPILE".

The 1970s were winding down and I was in my late teens when some fellow workers and I decided to get back to nature and become outdoorsmen. The desire came from being young, dumb, bored and stoned. What better place to begin than by hiking Mount Washington: the Rockpile, the tallest and most prominent mountain in New England. The early Native American tribes never climbed the mountain because they believed it was the home of the gods. That, combined with common sense, advised our native friends there was no possible benefit in going up that freakin' mountain.

On January 16, 2004, the summit weather observation registered a temperature of −43.6 °F (−42.0 °C) and sustained wind speeds of 87.5 mph (140.8 km/h), resulting in a wind chill value of −102.59 °F. That is colder than a well digger's kneecap. Even frozen refreezes at that temperature. Yvonne Jasinki writes in a Traveling Man article that about 70 years earlier, on the afternoon of April 12, 1934, the Mount Washington Observatory recorded a wind speed of 231 mph at the summit, the world record for most of the 20th century, and still a record for measured wind speeds not involved with a tropical cyclone. You can still see the chains on the original observatory hut that go over the roof and secure the building to rock to keep it from blowing off the summit like Dorothy's house in *The Wizard of Oz*. In the book *Where You Will Find Me*, it's mentioned that Mt. Washington is the sixth most deadly mountain in the world. It's certainly not that high in elevation as large mountains go, but the weather conditions are so unstable and unpredictable. Every jet stream, whether coming down from Canada, across from the west coast or up from the Gulf of Mexico seems to make a beeline straight for Mt. Washington.

These conditions came into play on our first attempt to summit. Take into consideration that back then the extent of your apparel consisted of a pair of Timberland work boots, blue jeans, and a down jacket. A few co-workers and I were bored when we decided to hike Mt. Washington. We had no experience, no training, and no proper gear. We started at the Pinkham Notch Center, hiking the Tuckerman Ravine Trail to Lions Head Trail and had gotten as far as the headwall when we were met by a person who looked like a Canadian Eskimo. This guy had crampons, an ice axe, goggles, and a full-face mask. With an authoritative voice, he instructed us to turn around immediately as there was a storm descending with white-out conditions. The tone of his voice carried a sense of urgency.

As he descended away from us, we had a pow-wow in which two of the five guys wanted to continue and two were undecided and I was the swing vote. With the image of Eskimo man still in my mind, common sense told me I didn't feel like dying that day. I suggested we turn back. I'll tell you I took quite a bit of heat for being a wimp from the two that wanted to continue, however within half an hour the temps had dropped, and those same two guys were taking off their boots to put their socks on their hands because they didn't have gloves.

Now far be it for me to brag, but they were going to be the first of several lives I would end up saving in the NH hills.

Second Attempt

The next year a different group of friends and I decided to camp out and give Mt. Washington another go. Again, five guys still wet behind the ears, green at the gills, with no experience or proper gear, heading up to the North Country.

The campout was a disaster as we had simply pulled in off a dirt road and camped in uncleared woods. We each had our own tent and gear, but because we all worked second shift, we slept in a little too late. I hate to admit it, but we were all partying and doing things you shouldn't do before hiking.

We set out on the same trail! Tuckerman Ravine to Lions Head.

We got off the trail and wandered into the Ravine only to be told by NH Fish and Game officer to take cover as they were blowing up an ice build-up at the top of the headwall. We hid behind boulders as pieces of ice the size of basketballs flew by like projectiles from the avalanche. Getting hit by one of those would have ruined the whole day.

After that fun, we started bushwhacking up the mountain. We were going up but not on any known trail. At one point I put my hand on a rock the size of an office desk and it slid backward about six inches. The three guys behind me were as white as ghosts with eyes like pie plates because they thought they were goners. They were shaking like a dog trying to pass a razor blade. A little later we had to cross a snowfield that was incredibly steep and ended at the edge of a cliff. We had no traction or poles or common sense. I was never so scared in all my life because one slip would be all you got. It was just plain stupid, and it is stunts like ours that cause deaths on Mt. Washington every year.

When we finally made the summit, I felt a rush of exhilaration and pride. The feelings vanished like a fart in a hurricane as we were greeted by a 60-year-old lady eating a hot dog. What the heck?

Oh yes, the joy of victory and the agony of the Cog Railway and Auto Road.

Anyway, crowds or no crowds, we did it. I had finally hiked my first of the forty-eight and didn't even know it. We ate some grub and headed down properly marked trails. We were tired but had the reward that only hikers can appreciate. As well as the inability to walk the following day.

2 THE STORY OF MT. LAFAYETTE
& MT. LINCOLN

Later that fall my work buddies and I decided to climb part of the Franconia loop.

Again, this is before the age of instant information, the Internet, cell phones, updated forecasts...that's right, kids, the Iron Head age.

We were still as clueless as a one-legged man chasing a donut down a hill, but we got a map and headed up the Falling Waters Trail. This was 40 years ago but if memory doesn't fail me there were four of us on this hike. When we got to the summit we were met by an unexpected white-out. This is really serious stuff, but back then we didn't know our butts from our elbows, so we just pushed on through the ridge trail to Mt. Lafayette. Due to the snow, the cairns along the knife-edge ridge trail were getting hard to find and we were starting to get cold. It was a disaster in the making. I'm amazed we never became statistics. Mt. Lafayette is the highest NH mountain outside of the Presidential Range. To make things more interesting, one of the guys we hiked with had a collapsing lung issue that, had it happened on the trail, would have meant serious poo poo. As I write this after completing the forty-eight with tons of modern equipment and the experience I've gained, I think back to these early days and wonder how we didn't die. I'm not kidding.

As we summited Mt. Lafayette, one of our crew got muscle spasms in his leg and could no longer walk. Did I mention we were in a white-out with no modern equipment or ways to call for help? Two of us got on either side of him and we managed to make our way to the Greenleaf Hut. He revived quickly and we descended along the Old Bridal Path. A memorable experience as we dodged a bullet on that one.

Thirty years later when getting ready to do the forty-eight, I had no desire to ever revisit mountains I had already done. I was in no condition to push that envelope.

On a side note, after getting married and having two wonderful kids, we as a family decided to hike Mt. Lafayette. The kids made it, leaping up the mountain like gazelles, but my wife and I stopped at the hut. She was done in and I stayed with her as her knight in shining armor. I never told her I couldn't have taken another step if my life depended on it. However, on the way down I saw something that I've never forgotten: a man and woman picking their way through the boulders of the Old Bridal Path in fine dress clothes. I mean the lady was wearing a dress and high heel shoes. SMH. It would be another ten years before I'd hike again. Those early friends would melt away as time passed and my life would change in big ways.

The gears of destiny started turning when Paul and Jane, my bother-in-law and sister, wanted to go hiking and they called the most experienced guy they knew. He couldn't go so they called me. Although Paul, Jane and I would hike Mt. Osceola and Mt. Moosilauke (and the four other mountains around Moosilauke), I won't relate those stories now since I hiked them again in pursuit of the forty-eight and they are mentioned later in the book.

3 THE STORY OF MT. CANNON

Mt. Cannon had been the famous site of the Old Man of the Mountain, a chiseled profile of a man's face formed by ancient glaciers. The profile was so famous that he became the NH State symbol. In May of 2003 the entire formation collapsed and slid down the mountain. A very sad day for NH.

Aside from being linked with the lost profile of the old guy, it is also well known for being a steep, difficult hike with lots of loose dirt on its trails. When Jane and Paul wanted to hike it, I said, "Sure, why not." Hindsight being 20/20, I would later come up with 35 reasons on one hand why not. I decided to extend the invite to my two kids, Janelle who was thirteen and Tim who was ten. The five of us geared up and headed north on I-93.

We decided to go up the Lonesome Lake Trail. It was a hot day and after a while, my kids started going at it. Bickering, fighting, complaining, whining... it was like watching me when I'm hungry. My family runs on its stomach. I wouldn't say we get hangry as much as it's a full-on Dr. Jekyll thing. My sister was quick to recognize the symptoms and suggested we stop and eat. After some sandwiches, the kids were miraculously transformed and began running up the trail with laughter and glee. I don't remember much of the hike, which makes me think it was so brutal that my mind has blacked it out. That happens often. Also, back then there were no cell phones for quick pics to remember things by.

I do remember that Cannon has a gondola ride to the top, so you meet all these non-hiker types that don't seem to belong on the top of a 4,000 footer. They were all admiring a view that they didn't work for. There really should be a law against that kind of thing. Either that or they should be required to bring cheeseburgers for the hikers.

On the way down, I remember experiencing a sensation that felt like my legs were on fire and someone was trying to put them out with a butcher's knife. The skin under my feet vanished and I was walking on pure nerve endings. Years later, as I began my quest for the forty-eight, that sensation would haunt me for the next 36 peaks. It didn't start to diminish until I only had eight peaks to finish. Don't let that discourage you from becoming a hiker because remember, I'm old and overweight.

Let me share tips on how you can begin to conquer the forty-eight.

First, read up on the history of the mountain you want to hike and find out how many people have died on it. Second, find out how many people got lost and were never found, or at least came limping out of the woods four days later nowhere near the trailhead they went in on. Then back away from those mountains as you are not ready for them. You don't want to become part of the 'hellarwe' tribe. Those are the hikers that appear out of the thickets saying, "Where the hell are we?"

Do what most people do. Start with the lowest elevations and the shortest trails and begin to work your way up. I guarantee you will end up with Mt. Owl's Head or Mt. Isolation as one of your last trips, but that's okay because by then you will have lost your senses and will think you're actually having fun out there.

Learn about the right equipment. What you need, what you don't need.

Learn what to pack. Hydration is more than water. You will need electrolytes, potassium, salts and pain relievers. Cheeseburgers are great to pack in. Oh by the way, if you're a nutritionist I don't want to talk with you as we have nothing in common.

Finally, do your research. There isn't anything you can't find on Google or YouTube. If, after your second hike, you realize you like what you're doing, drop everything and see a psychiatrist as soon as you can. Many of them now have offices located next to trailheads.

As I began my journey, I Googled, "What's the easiest 4,000 footer to begin on?"

It steered me to...

4 THE STORY OF MT. WAUMBEK

My thoughts are coming to me while I'm lying in a relaxing, hot, soothing bath that my wife, Darlene, ran for me. It's filled with magical salts and oils that are supposed to make me believe that one day I'll walk again.

Let me explain.

In 2012 I finally had all I could take of New England winters. Dark at 4:30 p.m., blistering winds, temps well below freezing, Northeasters dumping unbelievable amounts of wet, heavy snow... and that is just November.

The work I do would allow me to relocate anywhere in the country, but NH is home. It is where I was born and probably where I'll die. The State Motto "Live Free or Die" has been rephrased by the fine folks of this State to say, "Live, Freeze and Die".

I had to decide, move or find a way to somehow enjoy winter. I don't ski or snowboard because I'm too chicken of falling and breaking something that I prefer not to be broken.

So, at 54 years of age, I took up hiking in Pawtuckaway State Park which is literally in my back yard. Pawtuckaway has miles of trails and three small mountains: South Mountain at 900 feet, Middle Mountain at 800 feet and North Mountain at 1,000 feet. It is an ideal place to enjoy the great outdoors. I went online and bought hundreds of dollars of clothing that the experts said was required to enjoy the outdoors in any kind of weather. I also revisited a hobby I had enjoyed as a young teen and bought some snowshoes. I was ready for winter.

If I had only known the journey I was about to embark on would require the expensive gear I'd end up buying, I would have retired and then lived comfortably off the money I've spent on all the stuff you just 'have to have' to hike.

I hiked Pawtuckaway until I was known as "Pawtuckaway Ken". Well, not really, but I was having the time of my life hiking the winter doldrums away.

I had been extremely overweight. That's a nice way of saying that I was offered a job as the Super Bowl Blimp but turned it down because I don't like heights. (Put that on the back burner - remember; we're going to be talking about mountains.)

Within three winters of rushing off to the woods every chance I could and eating right, I had lost 50 pounds. I was in the best shape I'd ever been in 30 years.

I even hiked Mount Cardigan at 3,053 feet.

Then it happened - plantars fasciitis. The pain was worse than having to watch chick flicks with the wife. I couldn't even put weight on my right foot. For a year and a half, I was reduced to walking around with a limp. Other than the needle stick from hell in the form of a cortisone shot, nothing, including the shot, brought relief. For the next eighteen months, I had gotten depressed, gave myself over to watching TV and the wonders of junk food and mysteriously put all the weight back on. I couldn't understand how that happened. I was at a point so low I could have played handball off a street curb.

I finally decided that I would go to my church and ask for prayer. I don't know what you believe or don't believe, but I'm telling you that I asked for prayer for five straight weeks and sat back stunned as each week saw the pain level go down until it was totally gone. I really couldn't believe it, which is kind of sad because I'm the Pastor.

I initially tested my ability with a quarter-mile walk, then a mile, then two and before I knew it, I had taken to hiking again. I started eating right and was feeling good about myself.

Then it happened. From somewhere deep within my mind where psychologists would describe as the area that launches mid-life crisis, I got the idea that I would see if I could actually hike a 4,000 footer in New Hampshire.

I had heard from a friend of mine, Dave Salois, that he had been hiking the forty-eight. It was the first time I had ever heard that term and it was magical.

At 59 years old and 60 pounds overweight, I should have waited until after some conditioning, but why wait, I can do it!!! I asked Google what was the easiest of the forty-eight to begin with and that lying, no good, artificial, non-intelligent demon laughed and said "Mt. Waumbek".

I called my good buddy, Keith Tilton, and he agreed to go with me because he's retired and has little else to do. Keith is a life-long jogger who is in pretty good shape for an old man, and I was delighted that I wouldn't have to go it alone. My plan was, in case I met a bear, which I was now having extreme phobias over, there would be at least a 50/50 chance between who the bear would eat.

Off we went to enjoy the mountain hike. It was a beautiful August day. The forecast was for the high eighties with 90% humidity. If you don't know, as I clearly didn't know, what that feels like, imagine trying to breathe heavy, hot, unbreathable air while walking through the steam of a sauna. Now picture a rather steep incline, littered with impossible-to-navigate boulders and roots, that goes on for 3.7 mi. Times that by seven and add the heated ovens of hell and you are just about getting the picture.

We decided to take the Starr King trail to Mt. Starr King. At 3,900 feet of elevation, it would be a relatively level walk over to Mt. Waumbek. Within 200 yards from the car, I was already doubting I could continue. I was sweating so much that I was soaking wet from head to toe.

As we continued hiking for what seemed like an eternity, Keith was prattling on about some story and I was saying, 'Oh, oh, oh!" He thought I was interested in his babbling but really, I was saying, "O, O, O," which is the international sign for oxygen. Yes, that's right, I needed oxygen. This was like doing an Iron Man when you're only made from tinfoil. About three-quarters of the way up the incline from hell, my legs decided they didn't want to do this anymore, I almost quit. My mind had become confused with pain and I was getting delirious. I was actually praying for a bear to come and put a peaceful end to my existence. But I pushed on through the pain. Keith, who was enjoying the stroll, would later tell me how impressed he was at my determination. We hit a small rock formation, and I just leaned against it to rest and Keith thought I was throwing in the towel. I dug deep and pushed on. Then it happened. We summited. There I was, exhausted in the 80° heat and humidity smiling, thinking, "The worst is over." I'd like to go back up that mountain and slap the smirk right off my face!

After a protein bar and some water, I was ready to go home where I could cry and no one would see. We made short time of the next mile, then at Starr King, we began our descent. I was so naive, I was actually thinking, "I've got this." The next 2.7 miles, however, were a different story entirely. I had made it down a little farther when my thighs said, "Hey, fat man, we're tired of trying to hold you back from falling down this mountain like an avalanche. We're quitting." And then they quickly set the house on fire. What I mean by that is the burning sensation in my legs was unbelievable. Childbirth has nothing on what my legs were doing to me. Just when I thought things couldn't possibly get worse, it started raining. Okay, really it was puking rain; precipitation was nowhere in the forecast (welcome to the White Mountains!). Now you might be thinking that rain is a good thing when you're hot and overheated. But for those of you who wear glasses, you know what happens when you are always looking down in the rain: your glasses fill with water and begin to play optical illusional tricks on you. I couldn't tell if my next step was six inches down or sixteen inches down. I couldn't tell if the next rock I was aiming for was flat or angled. The situation became serious. My boots had filled with water and my wool socks had become like sandpaper that was now chafing both of my feet raw and causing a mild sensation known as torture. Still, we descended with me only making baby steps due to what I'll call being "mildly unconditioned". I was walking like I was on stilts because my legs didn't want to bend anymore. I offered Keith the keys to my truck and said, "I'll get down when I get down," but like the trooper and dear friend he is, he said, "No, I'll stay with you, I don't mind." Then he began yawning loudly behind me. How annoying can a guy get? All this time sweat mixed with rain was pouring into my right eye causing irritation and burning and swelling up to being almost closed. I looked like a prizefighter that had just seriously gotten his butt kicked by Mike Tyson. I drank 64 ounces of water and was still so dehydrated that I didn't pee for the next four days.

As we neared the parking lot, I was promising the good Lord things that I had never promised before if He would only get me back to my truck. Another hiker came upon us and Keith started talking the normal hiker jargon. I just made sounds like a dying sea lion, all the while looking like I had fallen off a mountain rather than hiked one. Well, I finally made it back to the truck and took off what felt like a 200 pound backpack, when Keith told me that his legs had started to get sore. I found that strangely amusing.

Here's a hiking tip: Recovery - when you try to get your heart rate and breathing back to something resembling normal!

So here I am lying in a hot tub filled with magical salts and oils that are trying to make me believe I will one day walk again when suddenly, a strange smile of satisfaction came from deep within my heart and a soft thought came into my mind, "But you made it!"

Oh, for those of you who think that these wonderful New Hampshire trails are hard-packed gravel, imagine climbing 4,000 feet while constantly picking your way through boulders and roots. When hikers say they are going into the woods for R&R, what they mean is Rocks and Roots. Really, someone should do something about that!

Also, if you're looking for the reward of a spectacular view, forget it! As one hiker reported, "Waumbek is surprisingly underwhelming."

And Keith actually expects me to do this again. SMH

And that, my friend, is hiking.

A great conditioning hike up Mt. Major today. Beautiful view and real windy. Does anyone in authority know how steep that freakin' thing is at the top? And little children are allowed to climb that? What are parents thinking?

Hopefully doing Mt. Jackson soon.

A quick scramble up North Mountain in Pawtuckaway Park on a beautiful morning. This is the delusion of conditioning which means absolutely nothing when you start up a 4,000 footer.

5 THE STORY OF MT. JACKSON

After barely surviving Mt. Waumbek, I started thinking about trying another 4,000 footer. Why? Because it's there? NO! Because a psychological phenomenon known as going completely nuts takes place when you start hiking these mountains. It becomes an addiction, a disease. Someone needs to start a support group or something. I would say a twelve-step program, but as soon as you start hearing the word "steps", your mind is on a steep rocky trail somewhere.

I had mentioned that I was beginning to get over my phobia of bears. I have since realized bears are smarter than humans when it comes to climbing 4,000 foot mountains. They live in the valleys and feast off trash cans and tell bear stories to each other about the stupid people they see hiking straight up these mountains. I also learned that if I don't watch "bear eating people" movies on Netflix, I'm usually a lot calmer.

New Hampshire is the natural habitat of black bears. They are smaller than grizzlies, brown and polar bears. That's good; however, nationally more people are maimed and killed by black bears than any other type of bear. That's bad! I also learned that black bears do not like the smell of human excrement. If I ever happen to see a black bear, I believe he'll stay away from me for that same reason because I will probably crap my pants.

As I began to select my next executioner, Mt. Jackson caught my eye.

Mt. Jackson is not named after the US President from the 1800s but for an outdoorsman who was totally a loner, psychotic and wanted to make sure no one ever followed him up to his favorite mountain. Little did he know that decades later some nut jobs in the world would take that as a personal challenge.

Of course, I was very apprehensive about subjecting myself to a repeat of my last experience, but this hike turned out to be spectacular. The cool and sunny weather conditions were ideal, unlike normal NH weather. There is a reason this area is called New England: its weather patterns are very similar to England, a dreary place where people go crazy from rain and a lack of sunshine. A doctor had told my wife that anyone who lives north of Boston, MA should take Vitamin D daily because our bodies don't get enough of it from too little sunshine during the winter. I figure God was smiling on me this day because He knew if I didn't have a good second experience I'd never come back.

The previous physical conditioning hikes I had done paid off with great rewards. I was actually deceived into thinking this trip would be fun.

I have quickly learned that, as you hike, you discover new gear that you just gotta have. This never stops and can lead to some marital issues if you don't know how to disguise your purchases. My new equipment purchases this time were hiking poles and a sweatband. A friend, who is quite a hiker in her own right, had told me about hiking poles. I had seen people who used poles, but they always seemed like older folks. A quick look in the mirror told me I'd fit right in.

Poles save so much energy and alleviate stress on your legs and knees, so your grunting only starts halfway up the mountain rather than 200 feet from your car. My son, Tim, who is a member of the Tahoe Nordic Search and Rescue Team told me if I was going to get poles, to spend the extra money and get the ultra-light carbon poles. I went with Black Diamond Carbon Z-Flex poles. My son didn't tell me I'd have to take out a second mortgage to afford them. I'm spending a lot of money to get a $4 patch, but I know it will be worth it and I'll wear it with pride. That's the spin I use on my wife, Darlene, to justify my purchases. She just smiles and takes out more life insurance. Tim also told me about the great deals that could be found on the Steep and Cheap website. Little did I know that I alone would give them their best fiscal year in a long time. I chose a U-band sweatband. It's reasonably priced at only $5.00 or so and made of a material that absorbs, disperses, and then dries the sweat off your forehead. Now if they could make one that also burned fat, they'd really have a winner. I usually don't put the sweatband on until I'm really starting to sweat. More times than not, that's between six or seven hundred feet from the car.

We took the Elephant Trail to the Webster Jackson Trail, five miles round trip.

The ascent was pleasant, and I noticed my breathing was a little better. That's to say I wasn't attracting any moose in heat. There were a couple of little stream crossings and a couple of areas known as "boney". That's a hiker term meaning "there are so many boulders in the trail that normal people who like their ankles usually turn around."

I wish somebody had advised me that the summit of this peak requires hand-over-hand climbing up an incredibly steep rock; quite frankly, it scared the daylights out of me. I had visions of slipping, falling, breaking a leg and dying on the mountain. I didn't know why I'd die; I just knew I would. I think it's a mild reaction to unaccustomed amounts of adrenaline mixed with a panic attack.

Am I missing something? Isn't there supposed to be a difference between hiking and climbing? My son insists that I'm hiking and not climbing but this sure felt like climbing to me. I'm guessing the other mountains couldn't possibly be this difficult. One nice hiker we met was from India. When he got to the cliff I just mentioned, he calmly turned and headed back down. I felt bad for him as he was only two or three hundred feet from the summit, but at the same time, I was giddy that I did something that a rational thinking person wouldn't do.

To summit on a clear sunny day is a reward in itself. The views were spectacular. We took some pics as souvenirs to gloat over in the future.

I was very concerned about the descent, but it went a little easier than I expected. Halfway down the never-ending trail, I mentioned to my hiking buddy, Keith Tilton, that my legs were getting sore. He informed me that his legs were not sore, they were just tired. Hmmm, I looked up tired in the dictionary and found there's a special note for hiker's jargon where "tired" means 'my legs are killing me so bad I think they're going to fall off'. From that point on, whenever we hiked and my legs seized up like cement on a hot day, I would mention that my legs were also getting a little tired.

By not drinking, we completed the ascent without too many stops and came down with even fewer. Hydration was a costly lesson which would come later in my experience. Still, I was quite proud of myself as I made a good showing. I mean, sure people passed me, but the look of sorrow in their faces towards my haggled, pathetic condition, let me know that other hikers are decent, caring people. They are also good-humored because as soon as they vanished around a corner, I could hear them laughing in hysterics.

After the two-hour drive home your legs kind of go into a state of shock and when you try to get out of your car, they turn into Jello that is the flavor of pain.

The good news is I only have forty-one 4,000 footers left. "Hahaha!"

People always say, "The views are breathtaking" No, the hike is breathtaking. The views are awesome.

Although we take a lot of pictures, I've found when you're 60 pounds overweight there's no amount of "sucking it in" that's going to make you photogenic.

You will notice that in the course of these adventures my excess weight shifts from 60 to 40 pounds. There are two explanations: First, it depends on what the voices is my head tell me on the day I am writing. Second, as I hike, I sometimes lose weight, then I celebrate by eating. The struggle is real folks.

And that, my friend, is hiking.

6 THE STORY OF MT. TECUMSEH

Mount Tecumseh is named after a Shawnee Indian Chief. I looked up the name Tecumseh in the dictionary and it said it was an ancient Indian word meaning "tortures old-fat-white man". That description hit the nail on the head, both for me and the trail. At 4,003 feet, Tecumseh just barely makes the height requirement but still gives quite a workout. Recently the height of Tecumseh was lowered to just below 4,000 feet. The removal of those last five feet makes all the difference in completing this hike. It's so much easier now.

Keith and I decided it had been a few days since we did something stupid, so I said, "Let's get up before any sane rooster and climb a 4,000 foot mountain."

No two-hour drive north would be complete without a stop at Dunkin's. Blueberry is my flavor of choice these days. Hopefully, the caffeine kicks in right around the time the trail starts getting steep. I'll take all the help I can get.

Being a novice at hiking 4,000 footers my plan was to look at maps and start with the easiest and end up with the ridiculously scary ones like the Presidential Range or the Bonds. I'm just not ready to do 24 miles. I figure after about 20 mountains I will have lost enough of my mind to venture out to the tougher ones.

It was a beautiful day and we geared up and hit the trail. My knowledge of what to pack was just starting to grow. The AMC always reminds people of the Ten Essentials:

1. Navigation - map of area and compass with a knowledge of how to use them

2. Sun Protection

3. Extra Clothing - especially a rain jacket

4. Light - headlamp

5. First Aid Kit (for me, ibuprofen is a must)

6. Fire Starter (ok, so here I want to share a little secret I learned from a former Green Beret - cotton balls coated with candle wax are extremely light and burn like crazy for about 4 minutes)

7. Repair Kit and Tools (an extra set of lungs)

8. Extra Food

9. Extra Water

10. Emergency Shelter (apparently staying at the Mount Washington Hotel doesn't count)

This is great advice and should be adhered to even by the most casual hiker. No need being careless and causing NH Fish and Game to mount another rescue.

Back to the hike.

We headed up the Mt. Tecumseh Trail. The first mile was a pleasant walk through a picturesque forest as the morning sun was filtering down through the trees. It was a set-up. The next mile and a half went straight up at an unbelievable pitch. Part of the way someone built steps going up. I don't know who did that, but I am eternally grateful. I think Led Zeppelin got their idea for "Stairway to Heaven" from this hike. It wasn't long before my tongue was hanging out like a panting dog in a desert. Around this time is when the question "Why?" surfaced. I have no good answer, but I know there is a mental time-warp that happens within hours that causes you to blackout the previously experienced pain. It's a hiking thing.

A 72-year-old guy passed us on the trail. Guys like that are jerks, not caring that their abilities are unfair to mildly unconditioned people like me and made me feel like I needed a safe place with cocoa and a puppy. Keith was happily impressed and said, "Soon we'll be hiking like that also." He's so funny. I don't mind being passed, but when people on crutches or three-year-olds go by, it's a bit much. Come on folks, there's a fat guy here with feelings.

We grunted onward until we finally summited. Oh, the joy and exhilaration that only Sir Edmond Hillary and I now shared! Someone once said, "You don't conquer mountains, you conquer yourself." Well, let me tell you, I just gave myself a huge butt whipping.

We had some trail grub. Trail grub is different than other food that normal flatlanders eat. I don't know why, exactly, other than you're eating it on a trail, and it seems a little more adventurous. We took some pics and headed down when Keith started whining about wanting to go .6 miles out of the way to a lookout. Sure, what is adding another 1.2 miles to a 5-mile hike. The things I do to stop the pouting.

I couldn't believe my eyes when I saw that some sane, realistic thinking person had built a bench chair at the lookout. The joy of taking a load off the legs and sitting for a while was worth the extra 1.2 miles. On the way down, we encountered a large group of 25 cheerful women who were from all over the country, all hiking together. Weirdos. They actually do this as some kind of hobby. Why are they not in pain? Why are they laughing and talking?

HOW are they talking? I can't even breathe! Later we ran into three more ladies who were happily chatting and laughing, not even panting or sweating. I smiled and said, "Enjoy your hike!" Really, I was hoping they'd meet a bear.

There's something about fatigue that makes the mind go to all kinds of dark places. I'm normally a fun-loving, likable guy, but pain bends the mind. I know the Marines say, "Pain is weakness leaving your body," but honestly it felt like the pain was moving in and building a retirement home. Finally, we got back to that useless mile at the beginning that I now know was only added for distance. Who would do that? (Let the reader understand that these easy five-mile hikes are setting you up for the ten to fourteen miles that most hikes will require.) I'm not even going to mention the physically gifted who do traverses and cover 27 miles in one day. My hat goes off to them but they're not normal. I'll bet they don't even eat pizza.

Again, Keith said his legs were tired (trail jargon for my feet, knees and thighs are have turned into oatmeal). We got to the truck and headed home, fastest time yet on a 4,000 footer.

When I got home, I went to get out of my truck when my legs said, "What do you think you're doing old man?" Oh yes, my legs talk to me and it usually isn't nice. Oh, the pain! My legs just didn't want to do anything resembling walking. I went inside where my wife Darlene caught me trying to inch my way down the stairs one agonizing step at a time. She said, "You look sore." I smiled and said, "Nah, my legs are just a little tired."

And that, my friend, is hiking.

7 THE STORY OF MT. HALE

It's 8 p.m. and I'm heading off to bed. Yup, that's right, bed! Let me try to explain. Darlene and I went to Jekyll Island, GA so I could perform a wedding for a friend and add in a few days of R&R. During that time, I did nothing but sit around and eat while my good hiking buddy, Keith, climbed Mt. Cannon. Because I wasn't there, I can't prove he hiked the whole thing with a smirk on his face, but I'm betting he did. After all, he was crossing a mountain off his list while I was not. So, feeling a little "one-upped", as soon as I got back, I said, "Keith, let's climb a mountain." (Oops, I mean "hike" a mountain.)

Now for eight days, Darlene had been telling me, "Go ahead and have another bacon cheeseburger, you're on vacation". (I'm going to have to see if more life insurance has been taken out on me.) So, I went to bed at 8 p.m. and set my alarm for 5:15 a.m. ON MY DAY OFF!!!

I had trouble getting to sleep because Darlene couldn't sleep and was turning over and over like a load of clothes in a Kenmore on spin cycle. After two hours I got up and took a melatonin all-natural sleep aid. Would someone please mark the bottle to inform you it doesn't kick in for five hours? I got up to the screeching of my alarm clock only to discover I was still so drugged I couldn't walk straight. I fought it off by splashing ice cold water on my face, got dressed, gathered my gear and left to pick up Keith. First stop, Dunkin's to get a coffee. Again, would someone please tell the lady at Dunkin's that "regular" has sugar? Dear Lord, how can a guy hike without sugar? The bitterness of the coffee along with the melatonin made me feel nauseous and lightheaded. Just as we arrived at the Mt. Hale trailhead, it started raining. Great, out come the rain jackets. I believe a rain jacket is one of the most important items to carry while hiking. They pack small and can be used as a windbreaker to stop windchill or keep you dry after you discover that weathermen flip coins to determine what the weather will be. Keith put on his new rain poncho and with his brimmed hat I was waiting for a cigar to come out and hear him say "Reach!". He really is quite a character. Instead, he said, "Quit whining and keep hiking."

We took the Hale Brook Trail. Most of these early hikes are just barely over 4,000 feet. We were doing the process known as conditioning. That means you're just trying to survive the lowest, shortest distanced hikes to start off with to see if you'll survive the longer trips. I've heard of some people saying, "I just completed my first 4,000 foot climb up Mt. Washington." Congratulations! I did it too when I was young and in shape. Those days are gone.

We knew that the rain clouds would sock in the mountain, but it didn't really matter as Mt. Hale doesn't have great views anyway.

The mountain is named after the famous historian, writer, and minister Edward Everett Hale. Mr. Hale was a powerful anti-slave proponent during the time of the Civil War. He and I have so much in common: both ministers, both writers. Edward went to Harvard at age thirteen, the same age I graduated from second grade.

Mt. Hale is 4,054 feet in elevation and one of the shortest hikes at four and a half miles. It's a great confidence booster.

The first .8 mile, I maintained my breakneck speed. I credit that to adrenalin. I thought, not bad for eight days of idleness and bacon cheeseburgers. We stopped for a short rest and some water but when it was time to go my body, loaded with melatonin, said, "Hahaha, what do you think you're doing?" I was dead. With two miles and about 2,000 feet of elevation gain left to go, I coined the infamous line... "What the Hale?" I honestly thought I would have to turn back as I could see the mountains on either side looming like giant grim reapers through the foreboding fog. Hiking is all about self-discovery and what I was beginning to discover about myself was that I really freak out when I think I'm about to die.

My pace was now like a turtle with a broken leg. You will find when hiking that some days you perform well and other days you just seem a bit off. A lot of factors affect performance: sleep, food, hydration, weather, and confidence. Having no confidence after stuffing my face and sleeping poorly, my hike in the rain was becoming a washout. I kept apologizing, putting one foot in front of the other, all the time complaining to Keith. His yawns were starting to get annoying, but he said, "There are no trophies for first; better slow and safe." What a pal! Those words gave me the courage to slow down even more.

The trails in these mountains are amazing. The NH woods are rugged and weather-beaten, aspects that give them a beauty all their own. It is truly refreshing to the soul. John Muir, a naturalist who was credited for influencing President Roosevelt's decision to make National Parks to preserve America's beauty said, "Come to the woods, for here is rest. There is no repose like that of the green deep woods." No words could be truer of the White Mountains. Except for the 'rest' part.

After hiking in the rain for quite a while, my head began to clear. We finally summited just after a young couple passed us. (Young people shouldn't be allowed to hike on the same day as old farts like Keith and me. It's demoralizing.) At the summit of Mt. Hale is a gigantic pile of rocks and the footings of a former fire tower. As I was scaling the rocks, I was wondering who in their right mind would want to climb a 4,000 foot mountain every day to work in a fire tower?

As any seasoned hiker knows, it's not about the adventure of the summit as much as it's talking about all the cool new purchases you've made. I was now the owner of a new hat with a large bill to keep the sun or rain off my glasses. Hiking with glasses is challenging and puts you in a tougher category than those who don't hike with glasses. Those who don't wear glasses can never understand what you go through, so I've learned not to mention that I'm hiking with a handicap that would equal the hassle of ten extra pounds in your pack. I also bought a new pair of Columbia nylon hiking pants with the cool pockets on the thighs. The unimaginable price tag almost made the pockets not worth it but who am I kidding? They are full-blown Crocodile Dundee. Darlene was not impressed and mentioned something about me having to look for a part-time job. Haha! That's funny! If I had another job when would I have time to hike? She's a keeper though. She even bought me a set of NH White Mountain maps with all the trails marked on them. Funny though that some trails seemed to be erased with new one's dead-ending in the Pemigewasset wilderness.

Keith and I started heading down because we were soaked like rats and a little chilly. I felt the serious hiking condition of hypothermia setting in. Some people say it's a peaceful way to die. Does that even make sense? There's a peaceful way to lounge, and a peaceful way to listen to tunes, but a peaceful way to die? Who comes up with this stuff? Did some guy actually freeze to death and then come back and say," Hey, you know what? That was really peaceful." I'm told that most people die from hypothermia because they don't know when to turn around. I usually get that feeling about 500 feet from the parking lot. Anyway, pay attention to forecasts including wind speeds and always bring extra layers of clothing, especially pants with cool pockets on the thighs.

We only stopped twice on our decent for less than a total of two minutes. Just enough to rest the legs and drink some water. As the decent from Mt. Hale turned into the decent from the abyss, my legs once again reminded me of the ice cream Darlene talked me into eating on vacation. All I can say is thank God for ibuprofen and ice packs.

Tomorrow I am officiating at another wedding and praying I'll be able to walk. A minister walking around like Frankenstein doesn't make for good wedding videos.

There's a funny thing that happens after hiking a 4,000 footer. That night when I closed my eyes to sleep, my mind kept playing memories of the rocks, roots, and trauma of the trail. I think it may be a mild case of PTSD. I couldn't shake the images until the next morning when I got my maps out and start sizing up the next mountain.

And that, my friend, is hiking.

8 THE STORY OF MT. PIERCE & MT. EISENHOWER

A friend once informed me that prior to doing a long, strenuous hike you want to eat carbs before the hike and protein after. So last night I loaded up with a large pepperoni pizza with extra sauce. I figure if I'm going to carb up, then I am going to carb up!

Well, that was as dumb as frying bacon in the nude. The pizza didn't set easy and caused a miserable night's sleep, not to mention a bit of a stomachache. I awoke sharply at 4:15 a.m. after a fitful night's sleep. I was staggering around like the zombies in *The Walking Dead*. I wanted so much to just sit for a while but I still had to gear up so we could leave at 4:45 a.m.

I was picking up David Salois, one of those guys who is three mountains shy of completing all forty-eight yet has hiked Eisenhower more times than he can remember. (He's hiked a number of the forty-eight numerous times.) For fun, he rides his bicycle 75 miles in one outing. Who does that? And why? David has been a lifelong runner and even ran a marathon. In my world... he's a freak of nature. Why he wanted to hike with me is beyond reason. It would be like Tom Brady working out with Larry the Cable guy.

We met at Rotary and hit it off because he had been hiking the Whites and was looking for new hiking partners. I had been hiking Pawtuckaway State Park with three mountains 1,000 feet and under. There is this thing in the world of hiking know as being somewhat evenly matched with your fellow hikers. This was not it! When Dianna, our church administrator, heard I was hiking with David, she said, "Well I hope you ate your Wheaties." (Wait a minute, isn't that what Bruce Jenner ate?) Anyway, everyone kept asking me, "Are you crazy?"

This double summit was going to be a nine-mile hike. First Mt. Pierce at 4,320 feet then over to Mt. Eisenhower at 4,767 feet, higher and longer than anything I had ever done. For me it was as forbidding as if someone had asked me to scale Mt. Everest. These peaks are part of the Presidential Range. The big boys. The mountains that people die on. Of course, my good hiking buddy, Keith, was going, but he is 70 years old. I knew if anything happened to me, he couldn't carry me down on his own. So, was I crazy for going on a hike with David? Yup, like a fox! To me, David was the next best thing to hiking with the NH Search and Rescue Team itself. He didn't know it, but he was my lifeline, my "phone a friend" if mayhem struck. We set off and I must admit we had the best time with the least stops ever. Conditioning is starting to pay off. The other day I noticed swelling on the front of my thighs and started getting concerned. Right before I called the doctor it dawned on me that what I was seeing was called muscle definition. I thought I was dreaming but my muscles were increasing. Freaky! Normally I look like Gru with the pencil-thin legs in *Despicable Me*.

We headed up the Crawford Path to Mt. Pierce and Mt. Eisenhower then down Edmands Path.

It was a gorgeous day, and no one seemed to mind that I was stopping every fifteen minutes to catch my breath and recover my heart rate. The conversation was congenial and the woods spectacular. The woods have a way of making the world feel right.

After hiking up Mt. Pierce for a short while, I heard David say from behind me, "Gee, I never hiked with a guy who wears white socks." I didn't know what to think about the comment until I turned around to see David's now-infamous poop-eating grin. I call it the "Salois' grin". Oh boy, it was on. That started a relationship of constant jabs and barbs and busting each other's chops. I wish I could bring out the best in him the way he can bring out the worst in me. He's even gotten Keith into the action and Keith, up to this time, was one of the nicest guys I'd known. The speed of Keith's corruption was instantaneous. No matter, I don't let that kind of stuff bother me. It's all in fun and anyway I give as good as I get.

Dave wearing the "Salois grin"

We summited Mt. Pierce and after soaking in the views and taking some pics, headed off to Mt. Eisenhower. The trail descended a bit then went up a picturesque ridge to the summit. Hiking above tree line is an amazing thing. It's almost like being on another planet. It's extremely rugged and beautiful all at the same time. Your views are unhindered in every direction and the blue shades of the surrounding mountains are mesmerizing.

My new purchase for this hike was a Columbia hiking shirt that is made of ripstop, fast-drying nylon and yes, it has pockets on its pockets. There is something about the gear that makes a fashion statement that says, "I'm a hiker! And I'm going broke."

As we approached the rocky summit of Mt. Eisenhower, the wind was somewhere between 30 to 40 m.p.h. At one time I thought I saw the wicked witch of the west fly by riding a bicycle. Man, these winds can rip up here and 40 m.p.h. isn't half of it. The wind is something to take into consideration when looking at a weather forecast because windchill can change a day hike into a nightmare real quick. I found out that hikers get into more trouble with hypothermia on the way down a mountain than any other time. Mostly because they are damp from sweat and no longer creating the BTUs for heat as they did on the way up. Even though windy, Eisenhower was amazing, sunny with blue skies.

When you stand on the rocky barren summit above tree line, you get the feeling that you are in a place that does not naturally sustain life. It is untamed and untouched. Though there may be thousands of eyes below looking up at the beauty of these peaks, there are only a few dozen looking down. Only those who love the call of the mountains can understand. Dave always reminds me that we are seeing what only one percent of the population ever sees. Strange. One percent is also the statistic of those who are mentally ill.

Even though I always say I am a one and done kind of guy, Mt. Eisenhower is a mountain I would consider hiking again. Little did I know that this is exactly how the disease of hiking addiction starts. Well, tons of pics later, we were resting and eating lunch when we realized we were right next to Mt. Monroe. It was right there clear as day. It was overwhelmingly enticing, like the song of the Sirens in *Homer's Odyssey*. Multiple, well-worn trails were all calling us onward. It was a tough decision not to go for it until the map showed us that "right there" was really a mile and a half away. These mountains are huge, and distance can be deceiving. It was an easy call to make as David and Keith couldn't stand my crying any longer. Dave said, "Please stop your whimpering. It's embarrassing."

We headed down in great time. The descent is an interesting part of a hike. Sometimes it can be more strenuous on the body. Edmond's Path trail is nothing more than a pile of twisted rocks calling out for twisted ankles. There was one place that was technical and wet, and Keith took a bit of a tumble. He seemed all right. We gave him some Kleenex for the tears, and a Winnie the Pooh band-aid for his scratch. The joy of summiting and the speed of going downhill made it a special time. The trees were in foliage and we drank in the view of the valleys below. When we hit the flat part of the trail, I turned on the gas. My legs were killing me, but I just wanted to get far enough ahead where I couldn't see David and Keith just so I could yell back, "Are you guys coming?"

I let them catch up and pass me just so I could get behind them and start yawning. Hahaha, white socks my a$$. Darlene says I have to apologize. She has no idea of the constant ribbing I put up with. It is all about who you hike with. I have met so many wonderful people on the trails; often they are passing me, so I don't talk to them.

David and Keith are a couple of great hiking buddies, and we truly had a great day with perfect weather, even though I thought I heard them making plans in whispers to hike again… without me.

And that, my friend, is hiking.

9 THE STORY OF MT. WILLEY, MT. FIELD & MT. TOM

Last week after summiting Mt. Eisenhower, our newly-acquired hiking buddy, Dave told us of a triple summit hike that was a lot of fun, but a "little steep". It has taken me some time to realize that when David says steep it means it's comparable to the Dawn Wall on El Capitan.

After making all the plans, David told us he had to work that day. Now when an avid, experienced hiker tells you of a hike that's steep and then pulls the work card, you know that you've just been set up and you are now going to hike Armageddon.

The old fella, Keith Tilton, brought his truck and I brought my car with my 27-year-old son, Tim. Tim lives at 6,000 feet in Truckee, California. He snowboards constantly and has hiked 14,000 foot peaks. He is super-conditioned just like his old man. When we arrived at the trailhead, Tim had a little bit of an attitude. That's the last time I'll ask him to carry my pack. Jeepers, Darlene carried him for nine months, you'd think he'd have been more appreciative.

Ken & Tim

As soon as we stepped out of Keith's truck, we immediately started going up at a 35° grade. That is steep enough for roofers and firemen to pee themselves.

We went up the Kedron Flume trail to the Willey Range trail. I have since found out that some less ambitious hikers hike up the other side of Mt. Tom, over to Willey, then back out the same way to avoid the steepness that we endured. The whining and complaining started and went on for some time. After about 20 minutes Tim and Keith asked me to be quiet. Sheeesh, some people.

We came to a place where ladders had been built into the side of the mountain because hikers don't usually carry pitons, hammers and rope.

This trail was rated easy to moderate by somebody who obviously smokes funny stuff. I would have much rather scaled a telephone pole. This was by far the most difficult trail we had done to date. Around this time, Keith and I were gasping for air while listening to a beautiful little song that Tim was whistling as he ran up the ladder system to take our pictures. Kids these days! I do want to give a shout out to all the volunteers who maintain these trails and who built the ladder systems. (Next time, if you could upgrade them to escalators, it would be greatly appreciated.) Seriously, you are the best!!!

We passed a couple of brave, middle-aged women who seemed to be struggling quite a bit. I brought my breathing down to where I could talk through my wheezing and said, "Keep going. You got this." They smiled and I thought I heard a muttered... "What a jerk!" I don't know why they'd have said that about Keith. They don't even know him.

After going about 76,000 feet we summited. Okay, maybe that's an exaggeration, it was only 73,000 feet.

We then crossed over to Mt. Field which was about 300 miles away. Okay, okay it was only 250.

On top of Mt. Field, we found some gray jays that came and ate right out of our hands. It was fun and entertaining and took my mind off the pain that was now ripping apart the muscles in my legs. After a while, I realized that those little jerks had eaten half of my sandwich. I jammed the rest of the sandwich in my mouth and started cursing the little rats out, but all Keith and Tim heard was "Mumphh, maph, moophal muggets!"

We crossed over to the last of three summits to reach Mt. Tom, and as we got to the top, my legs just didn't want to push anymore. I was coaching them like a maternity doctor to a woman 36 hours in labor, "Puuuuuuush." Tim had brought some Pedialyte for me. I think it is a type of Gatorade for babies. At first, I thought it was a joke, but as I was now starting to fit the description, I drank it.

DON'T DO IT! It tastes horrible. On the other hand, I have heard that chocolate milk is great for replacing everything your body needs. That along with a couple Whoppers and a large fries.

It was now time for our two and a half-mile descent as we went down the A-Z trail to the Avalon trail. Keith mentioned that his legs were getting tired. Now remember that is hikers' jargon for "three of my bloody toes fell off a half-mile back on the trail and my right ankle just snapped". I just smiled as my legs were getting tired also.

Tim, on the other hand, was skipping down the mountain like a happy little deer. I decided I would pick up a rock and teach him what it meant to hike with seniors. It was a good thing for him that I was in so much pain I could no longer bend over or throw straight.

Tim has a really expensive watch with an altimeter and weather station and NASA space launch control center. He told me that his watch had calculated that he had burned off 1,500 calories. For real? I'm pretty sure I burned that off by getting dressed that morning. Is that watch for real?

Of course, we met lots of other hikers and would always greet them with, "A fine day for a hike, isn't it?" which again is hiker jargon for, "I'm glad to see that I'm not the only idiot that's sending my leg muscles into crippling spasms."

Finally, we came out into the parking lot and I was amazed to discover that my legs didn't hurt. Unfortunately, it was because I no longer had any feeling from the waist down.

I can't wait for the day, like Dave, when I can say to some friends, "I know this awesome hike that you would love, it's steep," and then when they make plans to go, tell them with joy, "Oh, I have to work that day."

And that, my friend, is hiking.

Special note:

Recently it was Pastor Appreciation Day and the people had gotten together and bought me this mountain climbing watch just like my son's. It also has a GPS, altimeter, barometric pressure gauge, and a NASA launch center. I'll need to hire a Ph.D. in techno language just to program it. I think it also mounts to the bottom of your feet and carries you up the mountains. I am so excited. A great gift from the best congregation in the world.

10 THE STORY OF MT. GARFIELD

Mt. Garfield turned out to be my sweet sixteen on my journey to the forty-eight 4,000 footers. Ten have gone by the wayside since August when my original goal was to do one this year and then start next year. Not bad.

Mt. Garfield is named after the 20th President of the U.S. He was killed by an attorney. Probably just got his lawyer bill and had a heart attack. The hike is long with a steep section right before you summit and break the tree line.

Again, I was with my good hiking buddy, Keith Tilton. He had bought a truck just like mine, then a kayak like mine and now wants to complete the forty-eight. Oh well, imitation is the sincerest form of flattery.

With us was our new companion, David Salois, who had also invited an avid hiking friend, Sue, with her dog, Bonnie. It was a pleasure to hear woman sounds while hiking that for once were coming from a woman. We met Sue at the parking lot, geared up, and off we went. We were all in high spirits, even though the mercury in the thermometer had fallen so low it was laying on the ground.

Of course, I bought a new Adidas mid-layer hooded jacket as it was now autumn. I also switched over to a medium-sized pack I had bought years ago at the Kittery Trading Post. I didn't even know there was such a thing as a "woman's backpack". OK! So big deal that it's purple. I like it. It has lots of straps to lash stuff down on it. My hiking buddies immediately started talking smack about it.

I paid them no mind.

I won't mention how David was wearing a type of thin, stretchy beanie and sporting some growth on his chin. He also wore a black top, tan shorts and tan boots. He looked like a pirate on safari.

We took the Mt. Garfield trail ascending the 4,500 feet.

Now you need to know that the day before we had a mild hurricane in NH. No surprise that there were no other hikers to be seen. More experienced hikers knew what to expect, and they stayed in bed. What was supposed to be the trail was now a free-flowing river all the way to the top. To make it a little more interesting, there was just a hint of ice on the rocks closer to the top and, on the way down, we experienced our first snowfall of 2017.

We had to abandon a river crossing and go further downstream to find a bridge. A lot of time was spent in discussion and map searching (which lets you know you're hiking with professionals). We finally found the bridge, made the crossing and picked up the trail. In some places, the water was flowing so freely down the center of the trail that we were forced to hike on the edges. It looked more like a water park ride than a trail. I thought for certain we'd see some kayakers come down at any moment. There were also a lot of blowdowns. Those are trees that the wind has knocked over but that is not as cool as saying blowdowns. We found ourselves scrambling over, through, and under them.

We stopped and rested often. Thank God for Sue. She took the heat off my continual need to recoup from hyperventilation.

Keith runs five miles every other day because the voices in his head tell him to, and David rides his bicycle to NYC just for the food, and Sue has hiked the forty-eight twice, and I think she also hikes in her sleep.

That left me in competition for fourth place with Sue's dog, Bonnie. I sized her up and thought, "I got this."

Well, how was I to know that Sue had cloned a mountain goat and made it look just like a Cocker Spaniel? The worst part was the 'dog' kept passing me and then would fall behind only to pass me again. But what really got me going was the look in her eyes and the smirk on her face. I quickly told her in non-verbal mind-to-mind dog talk (yes, I know how to do that) that if she wanted to make it off the mountain alive, she'd better knock it off. I'm climbing (hiking) these mountains to get a patch that says you've done it. That little mutt has already got her patch. Oh, the irony! I thought of stealing her little bandana with the patch on it, innocently claiming that she must have lost it and ending my pain of hiking by declaring the patch mine.

I just kept reminding myself that I'm still 60 pounds overweight and, when I shed it, I will own that dog at hiking. Still, the dog smirked every time she passed me.

Keith mentioned wearing his "I'm with whiner" T-shirt once or twice. I don't see what's funny about that. I don't think his wife, Hazel, would like that at all.

I was wearing long johns and after a few miles I thought for sure I would melt. The team stopped long enough for me to squirm and

47

wiggle and shed them. I'll never do that again. The harassment I took was overwhelming. I guess it was a good thing there were no other hikers near us. There are some things on the trail that are hard to explain even to other hikers, but everyone knows, "What happens on the trail stays on the trail."

When we summited, we found the wind chill was so cold we couldn't stay long, the tears from pain were freezing on my cheeks. Keith started crying real tears saying that his ears were getting cold, and I didn't want the tears forming an ice dam on his cheeks. After all, who am I to point out someone's whining? The day was partly cloudy, and the sun was shining rays down on Owl's Head Mountain. It was breathtaking. We took lots of pics. One day, if you and I ever meet, I'd love to show you my 13,000 mountain pics.

I had now started carrying Gatorade. Grape is my favorite flavor. I find it replenishes electrolytes and other stuff. When hiking you need to think of these things because your body needs electrolytes and other stuff.

We made it down in record time (I was setting the pace), said goodbye to Sue, and headed for Dunkin's. More electrolytes… and stuff.

Keith said his legs were tired, but I noticed when he tried to get out of the car, he made deep sounds like someone getting their legs pulled off on the stretching racks of old England.

It's kind of embarrassing to hike with folks like that.

It was a great hike, one I thought I would never have been able to do. Not because of the challenge of the hike, but because David drove, and I never thought I'd see the light of day again… EVER!

I didn't know it was legal to do 85 m.p.h. while holding a coffee in one hand and texting with the other but, hey, who am I to argue legalities with a police officer?

With our legs still in tremors and twitching like an insect on a bug light, I found myself agreeing with David and Keith on doing another climb.

After dropping them all off and arriving back home, I tried getting out of my car and found that the stretching racks really do hurt, as I was now making the same sounds Keith had made.

And that, my friend, is hiking.

Oh, and if either one of them ever says I wear pink long johns, they're lying. They are blue. And thank God they were too far away to see the teddy bears on them.

11 THE PAWTUCKAWAY LOOP

Pawtuckaway is a beautiful NH State Park with miles of hiking trails. It is the most southerly park in NH and right in my backyard.

Our original plan for this particular day was to hike Mt. Flume and Mt. Liberty. However, the weather forecast was for a 22° temperature with 45 to 55 mile an hour winds and gusts up to 75 miles an hour, creating a wind chill of 30° below zero. Now God has given me the wisdom to know when something can kill me, and I'm partially allergic to dying. I'm always concerned when something can kill me. It took some persuasion, but I finally convinced these other fine gentlemen that I didn't want to die at this time. I investigated the possibility of Mt. Roberts in Moultonborough, and only about 2,700 feet, but the forecast was for 20° below. I settled for doing an eleven-mile loop in Pawtuckaway Park, and these other fine gentlemen agreed, after some subtle persuasions consisting of crying and foot-stomping.

I didn't bother telling them that I was feeling quite sick and running a fever. I won't even dignify that remark by telling you how high my temperature was. I also didn't mention that my pack was twice as heavy as everyone else's. What is the point? They all just roll their eyes, shake their heads and sigh. So, off we started with a new addition of Dustin Ramey, a friend from the Raymond Rotary Club, joining in.

For almost the entire trip I was walking point. This is the most dangerous position, because, by the time you find out a rock is slippery, you have already landed on your backside and re-sprained your right wrist; the other hikers now know to avoid or proceed past that area with great caution. It is a thankless job that usually falls to the most experienced, toughest hiker. Alas, I am much too humble to dwell on these finer points.

The weather was nice, and we had a fine hike. I didn't even mind all the jabs and digs that I was taking from the rest of the crew. There was, however, an unsettling feeling of why I enjoy winter solo hiking in Pawtuckaway, and why this hike was so much different. Oh, oh, the tranquility of being alone.

After missing one trail marker because the sun was in my eyes, Dave Salois took the lead.

The name Salois is Mic Mac for "runs like a greyhound".

Now David and Dustin are both former athletes and Keith, as I have mentioned before, runs five miles every other day. I, on the other hand, am old and overweight. When they put on their self-wicking, base layers, they look like models. When I put on my Under Armour base layer, I look like the Michelin Man. I must admit, I had quite a hard time keeping up. But I let them go on ahead because I figured their need for speed was due to wearing shorts, and they were freezing from hypothermia. They just needed to get the blood flowing. I just smiled knowing that I had the keys to my car and, no matter how fast they went, they would still have to wait for me. It's kind of evil, but it did bring a certain satisfaction.

As we started getting close to the end, they all started guessing how long they thought the trail was, which they unanimously guessed was under ten miles. With my wisdom and experience, I told them it was at least eleven to twelve miles. They chuckled and rolled their eyes until we reached the end; Dustin's Trip Finder revealed we had covered 12.8 miles.

What can I say? It's not the fastest who wins the race. Now I'm not going to say that I didn't have fun, or that they didn't put me through a grueling physical test, or that they didn't relentlessly pick on me while I was feeling under the weather, or that the extreme wind had blown a piece of debris in my left eye that irritated me for the entire hike, because hiking buddies don't do that.

Next time I think I'll do that 30° below hike.

And that, my friend, is hiking.

On always being prepared

The following story is not for the faint of heart. If you are the least bit squeamish, do not continue. Just skip this story and enjoy the rest of the book.

For most of my childhood, I grew up playing in the woods. In fact, one year, my brother and I camped out from late April through mid-October, in an old canvas tent we pitched in the woods behind our house. It was one of the best years of our lives which, is a coincidence, because our Mom said the same thing.

Anyway, in all my years of endless hours in the woods, from childhood to adulthood, I never once went #2 in the woods. I wish I could still say that!

At age 59, my introduction to "Does a wild man crap in the woods?" took place as I went for a late winter hike in Pawtuckaway State Park.

It was the time of year when portions of the trail were covered by patches of snow and ice, while other parts were bare rocks and gravel. I had hiking poles at the ready and was wearing my spikes and carrying a daypack with all the necessities. As I got about a mile in along the trail, a mild concern started to brew deep within my abdomen. (Not that I had done anything wrong, but as a word to the wise, don't eat burritos you buy at a gas station.) I paid no mind to the growing rumblings, like a kid who whistles while going past a cemetery. By mile two, things were happening that could no longer be ignored. The building pressure was strong enough to move tectonic plates. My mind kicked in with adrenaline tinged with a touch of panic. I remembered seeing only two other cars in the parking lot. Knowing that people come from all over the northeast to go bouldering in Pawtuckaway, I felt the odds were in my favor and not many hikers would be on the trails. Even if they were, Pawtuckaway is 2,300 acres, with miles of trails. Thinking fast, I knew time was of the essence as my internals were now doing flip-flops. I took a quick mental inventory of my supplies and knew I had a third of a roll to TP in my stash-bag. I thought I was prepared.

I also realized that, hikers or not, I needed to get off the trail. The countdown had begun, 10…, 9…, I saw some large rocks up an incline about 60 feet off the trail. 8…, 7…, I made a beeline towards them while sliding my pack of my back. 6…, 5…, I threw my pack on the ground, dug out the roll of TP, and began circling like a dog looking for just the right spot. 4…, 3…, I lowered my pants and undies and crouched down preparing for the unavoidable. 2…, 1…, I grabbed the roll of TP and clung to it like a 4-year-old with a teddy bear. 0…, Blastoff! I'm not exactly sure what happened next because I think I momentarily blacked out. There was one last violent tremor in my abdomen, my heart skipped a beat, and my sphincter surrendered with a whimper, followed by an ungodly roar. The thrust lifted me three inches off the ground all while remaining in the crouched position. When a rocket takes off, there is what is known as, blow-by. That is when the flames from the engine hit the ground and fan out in every direction. This blow-by was a flame of a different kind. I crouched, stunned and dazed as another three gallons drained out like lava from Mt. Butt-hole. I not only emptied my internals of a bad burrito but also of everything I had eaten in the last month. As the forest quieted down from the reverberations of the explosion, my mind began to regain focus. I slowly wiped some drops of sweat from my forehead and assessed the job that lay ahead.

Then I heard it. The sounds of voices. No! This can't be real. Wake up! Wake up!

I could just make out the forms of two hikers coming down the trail. I quickly prayed a silent prayer: Please let them be men and save me from total humiliation. The words no sooner left my thoughts than I heard a soft voice of the feminine gender. Oh, come ooooonnn! I was crouching on a small hill amongst the rocks with my pants down, trying with all the strength I had left to blend into the landscape. I don't know if they ever saw me, nor do I want to know. This is one reason I don't like hiking in bright colors. In fact, I wished I had been in camo. As soon as they disappeared, I began cleaning up on aisle six, seven and eight. Someone once said, "A job is not finished until the paperwork is done." Well, I used "ALL" the paper, a few old candy wrappers and a slow-moving chipmunk. I hiked the two miles out trying to process what had happened, as did the chipmunk.

The only positive takeaway was, I can never say I've never gone #2 in the woods again. I think I did #1, #2 and even a little #3 all at once!

Here's a big hiking tip, always carry TP. You just never know.

12 THE STORY OF MT. MONROE

Mt. Monroe is part of the Presidential Range and towers over most of the other forty-eight at a whopping 5,382 feet high.

We had thought about doing it when we were on Mt. Eisenhower, but it was a little too far and we were kind of spent. You must be aware of your limitations.

By this time, I had added to my new purchases a headlamp and some better first aid equipment. This was a real winter hike, so I also bought new gloves and socks and lots of hand warmers. I had no idea what I was getting into, but since I was the one that foolishly suggested, "Hey, let's do Monroe," I was in it for the long haul and what a haul it was! Meanwhile, I overheard Darlene on the phone with the funeral home inquiring about the costs of funerals these days. She's super thoughtful like that.

Once again, my partners in crime were Keith and David. There was a lot talk on the two-hour drive north, I think mostly from nerves. Finally, at one point, I think it was Keith that said, "For crying out loud, would you be quiet?"

"Well, excuuuuuuse me!"

Hiking the Ammonoosuc Ravine Trail, we started off at about 22° on snow covered ground. For the first mile and a half, it was a moderate hike - a trail rating that means, "you should have stayed in bed." For the last grueling mile and a half, the path went up at an unbelievable pitch; the snow and ice made it extremely difficult. Dave and Keith were showing off their new 5/8" microspikes. I, on the other hand, was wearing an old pair of 1/4 inch microspikes that served well for flat hiking. This was not flat hiking; it was scaling an iceberg with thick, deep blue ice. It actually had a haunting appearance, where we expected to see someone frozen beneath us. As I was crossing over a menacing, difficult section, I kept hearing a little voice that said, "Don't worry about descending, you're never going to make it off this mountain." At one point I experienced what (I hope) is the closest I will ever come to a panic attack; I had dizzy spells and was feeling nauseous and disoriented. The difficulty of the climb was intimidating, and I wanted to turn back. I kept slipping on steep sections, while Dave and Keith were moving along like two polar bears. When you slip on steep ice several things happen. Usually, you fall to a knee and that knee takes a pounding. Also, your muscles tighten like wound-up rubber bands, and you use valuable strength that I, for one, didn't have. But the worst is the panic of not knowing how much you'll slide. Some of these ice flows were 30 feet long. After you've slipped multiple times, you begin to question why you're there. The views were breathtaking. Literally! As I viewed how high we were and how cold it was, I was taking air in, but nothing was coming out. I really don't know what happened, because I've suppressed most of it. By now I was crying like a five-year-old facing the dentist's chair.

In the past, I have often thrown little jibs and jabs at my hiking buddies. But not today. Keith Tilton and David Salois were very encouraging and continually trying to talk me out of turning around. I think they felt that they had come too far to turn back just because I thought I was dying. They insisted that I stop and eat and drink. I had not been doing that and my blood sugar levels were whacked, and I was becoming dehydrated. That's my fault! I learned a big lesson: stay fueled up and hydrated. My son later scolded me, in a mind-warping role reversal, about drinking every half hour while on a strenuous hike.

When I finally stopped, I pulled out a partially frozen chocolate milk and drank the slush down. I also had a bit of a protein bar and felt the results immediately. I felt like Popeye after he ate spinach and like Rocky Balboa, I could hear "The Eye of the Tiger" playing in my mind.

Thankfully, we were only about 100 yards from the Lake of the Clouds hut; after reaching it, we were able to sit on some benches and eat a little more.

We met a couple of youngsters who were heading down after completing the forty-eight with a sunrise hike up Mt. Washington. They were very pumped, although my companions and I thought we could smell some whacky tobacky. Kids these days! SMH

As we were resting it began getting overcast and started snowing quite a lot.

The summit was only about a half-mile away, but David was now considering calling it and turning around. The possibility of losing the trail during a whiteout is a real threat and nothing to be trifled with. People die up here every year. I was against turning around because I felt I had endured too much to throw in the towel.

Just then another solo hiker came up and reassured us that this was a cloud burst according to the Mt. Washington Observatory's weather forecast.

Together we summited.

We took lots of pics and had some laughs at my earlier experience where I left lots of yellow snow.

I found out that going down was easier than I thought because I sat on my butt and slid down the ice. They may have laughed and threatened to take pictures, but, as long as I was going down, I could have cared less. I'm glad I completed the hike but winter hiking on these mountains is a serious event and I have learned a valuable lesson to stay hydrated and fueled. I don't know why Keith and David listened to my recommendation to climb this mountain in the first place. They should have known better than to listen to me. Also, the sign at the trailhead talked about hikers being in perfect physical condition. They should have been aware of my limited abilities. But I'm not holding that against them.

Darlene had made all three of us some dried apple slices and I was now enjoying mine. I won't mention that Keith and Dave's bags did not even make it past Concord on the trip up.

It was on this hike that I discovered that David is part Micmac Indian. That cleared up a whole lot for me. You saw the picture of him and me at the summit on the cover of this book. Can you tell which one is the old fat man and which one is the Indian? But, hey, I'm not holding that against anybody.

I really do appreciate these guys, and they were a tremendous source of encouragement that helped me to persevere and summit that mountain. Having good friends like this is what hiking is all about. I will say that if the roles had been reversed, I would have offered to carry their backpacks. But who is going to bring up a thing like that? Not me!

I've discovered a new phenomenon. The day after a grueling hike I feel fine. Walking, running up and downstairs... but on the second day?

And that, my friend, is hiking.

13 THE STORY OF MT. OSCEOLA

I am now a fan of Science. In school, next to Math, History, and Geography, Science was my worst subject, but I have recently become a fan. Let me explain why.

My good buddies, Keith Tilton and Dave Salois, wanted to go hiking because the weather was looking promising.

Another friend, Tim Mailloux, also wanted to give it a try, so the four of us loaded into my car and headed up to the Great North at 5:30 a.m.

Our first dilemma was that the road to Mt. Osceola was closed for the winter, so we decided to try the other side which was closer to the trailhead. Honestly, I don't know how three full-grown men all using the GPS on their phones can fail to give good directions, but it happened. After a few wrong turns, we arrived at the other side of the mountain only to find that road closed as well. The cheery response was, "It will only add another five miles to our eight and a half mile hike." OK... so an eight and a half mile hike will now be a thirteen and a half mile hike???

I said nothing. A good leader sometimes delegates and allows others to make decisions, even if they are bad ones. I hinted that we had passed a nice breakfast place, but there were no takers. Off we went up a two and a half-mile road that was steeper than most mountain trails. As David and Keith were sprinting farther and farther away from us, I began to feel I was on the Bataan Death March. I was soaked in sweat and breathing way too heavily.

I was wondering if something was mildly affecting me, like cancer or tuberculosis. When we got to the trailhead, I told them I was going to turn back. They could carry on without me. I know that without me, their hike would be dry, boring and monotonous, and that led to much debate, pleading, imploring and crying. I also think they just didn't want to piss off the guy with the car. Finally, I gave in and started to climb. It was that or freeze to death.

Watching three grown men realize they may not get a chance to hike is like watching a mom take away a Snickers bar from a five-year-old at the checkout. Most times the five-year-old gets over it quicker.

It was a laborious climb. Again, I couldn't put my finger on what was happening to me. Twice I stopped and begged them to go on without me and I would return to the car. I really felt bad because this was Tim's first mountain, and I didn't want him to miss it. Finally, they agreed. I was thrilled. I began descending at a nice enjoyable pace that would make any 90-year-old person shake their head in disgust. I was really loving the winter woods as my mind started wandering. Soon I started wondering what a black bear attack would look like. I don't know why I started thinking that, but the more I gave into my imagination, the more real it all started becoming.

At the height of this mental frenzy, I heard the tremendous thumps of a fast-moving animal coming up behind me. I jumped right out of my hiking boots and socks and they took off running without me. My heart stopped and I think I may have tinkled. Thirty seconds later my hiking poles came flying back to earth with a clatter.

The bear was smiling: it was Dave. I wanted to kill him, but I also wanted to hug him. Dave wouldn't let me hike alone. Though it was a nice gesture, I had a hard time explaining the brown snow at my feet. A real bear encounter would have been better! At least easier to explain the mess.

Anyway, I was perplexed at my lack of performance during this hike until I remembered that seven days before I had donated double reds. You know, red blood cells. The things that carry oxygen to your body. I remembered reading that it took 112 days to replenish reds after a donation. No wonder I couldn't seem to catch my breath. There was nothing left in my blood to carry the little donations of oxygen to my muscles. Sorry about getting scientific, but this was a real breakthrough that taught me to never donate blood again until this hiking stuff is over.

When I got home (after putting up with all the snide remarks on the trip), I looked up five different articles, and by golly, wouldn't you know that donating double reds can affect your athletic performance for three to four weeks. The Red Cross should have a disclaimer. No double reds if you're hiking 4,000 footers.

It affected other aspects of my life as well. I had asked Darlene why she married me, and she said, "Because you're so funny." I said, "I thought it was because I'm a great lover." She said, "See, you're hilarious!"

That's my scientific discovery story explaining why I had trouble hiking and I'm sticking to it. Not to mention that I was still fighting off a bad cold with a slight fever, and still I turned in a seven-mile hike to 2,700 feet of elevation.

Mt. Osceola, I'll see you in the spring! Even though I may have to find different hiking buddies who can appreciate science!!!

And that, my friend, is hiking.

Here is a note from Tim Mailloux on his first mountain experience:

Very interesting day, had a great time with some great men (even though one squealed a little - I won't mention any ..ah never mind... it was Ken Bosse). The summit was beautiful. The hike was great, despite the snow, the steep hills, the rocks, the ice, the downed trees, and the fog at the top... it was still a wonderful experience! And after my legs stop cramping up, I look forward to the next hike. I definitely give credit to these folks, each old enough to be my dad, but I still had a hard enough time keeping up. Great job, guys! I didn't think I'd be able to do the mountain after that long steep road just to get to the trail. It was horrendous. Pushing 70-years-old, Keith was a machine.

14 THE STORY OF MT. LIBERTY

After a couple of winter hiking fails, I got it into my mind to try for a third time. I was a little bit nervous because a lot was riding on whether I could successfully summit Mt. Liberty. It was Patrick Henry who said, "Give me liberty or give me death." If he had been speaking of Mt. Liberty, he would have just said "Give me death," because that mountain was a royal pain in the butt.

I started off at five in the morning with my good hiking buddies Keith, David and for the second time, Tim Mailloux.

Tim has a peculiar method of eating breakfast: he makes a sandwich, wraps it in tinfoil and sticks it on the manifold of my engine for the ride up north so he can eat a hot sandwich before the hike. Geeesh, hasn't he heard of Dunkin's?

The trail to the summit was a little over four miles with the option of crossing over to Mt. Flume which would add another mile and a half one way. Mt. Liberty is 4,459 feet high, and Mt. Flume is 4,328 feet high.

The trail was rated by AMC as being strenuous. That's a nice way of saying you must be a flipping idiot to try to climb this in December. But, off we went on another adventure.

My new untested gear (I'm really starting to look the part if it wasn't for being 50 pounds overweight) consisted of Marmot Scree pants that performed wonderfully (flexible, breathable, water-resistant and a cool logo that glows in the dark) and HillSOUND ice spikes that were amazing. They gripped like bear claws in a slow runner's butt.

Even with the spikes, there was a time during the descent that I went for a 20 foot slide down an ice-covered rock slab that left me covered in snow. "What did your hiking buddies do? "Were they concerned for your safety?" Well, their response was to laugh and say, "Did anybody get that on camera?" But I'll come back to that in a little while.

We hiked up the Liberty Spring Trail and we finally arrived at the top after an incredibly strenuous ascent. I had to stop numerous times. The other guys were upset because they said they could look down the trail and still see where I'd stopped the last time. Man, hikers can get crabby in cold weather when they're not moving. I was sweating like a dog and there they were doing jumping jacks. We found out the temperature had dropped considerably; a slight wind chill brought it down to somewhere between Antarctica and Outer Space. One website report said it was negative five degrees. Yeah, right, maybe in the car with the heat on! To say it was unbelievably cold is an understatement.

It became a race to layer up fast or freeze to death. I know there are a lot of hikers who take to the mountains in 40° below and lower, but I can't afford $250 gloves or $700 jackets. As it is now, Darlene had given me all my Christmas and birthday gifts for the next two years and I still needed stuff.

We finally made the summit. It was fun to remove your gloves to snap some beautiful pictures only to find out you had 30 seconds before frostbite set in.

It dawned on me that my survival gear is useless if my fingers won't work.

Mt. Liberty has a rugged peak and some amazing views. In the winter conditions, it was exhilarating.

Then came the time for the big decision. Do we push on and summit Mt. Flume or should I say Mount Doom! I'm sure I saw the fires of Mordor spouting from its top.

After amassing years of wisdom and mountain experience, I said, "I think we should go back," which, by the way, was a joint decision. I immediately started taking flak from Frodo, Samwise, and Gollum. I'll let you figure out which one was which because it really doesn't matter. But here's the truth you will probably never hear... as we started to descend, I took incredible ribbing over the decision not to summit Mt. Flume. However, in just a short time we discovered that all our hydration packs had frozen solid and we couldn't drink. Had we gone on to the other summit, I'm sure we would have started dropping from dehydration. What the other fine fellows may never admit is that my mountain skills and razor-sharp mind intervened to save their lives that day. But who would boast about a thing like that?

Even though it was frigidly cold, the views were a spectacular reward.

As we headed down, I found out that my Columbia bug-out boots - which had kept my feet toasty warm and had been a delight to wear while ascending - were now jamming my toes quite severely in the descent. I'm sure somewhere there is an evil empire that uses this as a form of torture. Like waterboarding for your feet.

When I got home and removed my socks, I noticed that my left big toenail had turned an awesome shade of purplish-blue. I'm sure I will lose the toenail; when I do, I will hike again, just to experience what it is like to not get my toenail jammed. I have now learned a little hiker's secret that I will share with you. Before descending, re-lace your boots. Tighten them as much as you can, especially around the ankles. It won't stop the jamming but will cut the blood flow, so your toenail won't turn blue. At least not until you get home.

While going down, thirsty and experiencing incredible pain, I was taking quite a ribbing from my fine friends (for whom, by the way, Darlene had made a nice batch of chocolate candy). But no sense in connecting their behavior to my kindness. I didn't let it bother me for I'm sure they were just jealous of my new mountain beard that made me look the part. If you're going to be a mountain man you need a beard. Darlene didn't like it because she was afraid it would alter my appearance too much should body identification be needed. Again, I had to take point all the way down which, as you remember, is the most difficult position and reserved only for the most skilled and experienced hikers. Ha! Actually, letting the slowest person take the lead is the kindest, most thoughtful way of hiking. I've heard of other groups that let the slow person fall behind. Then, when the faster hikers stop and let them catch up, they start the hike again, so the slower hiker never gets a rest. If you find yourself in that situation, you may want to find other people to hike with.

All in all, it was a tremendous hike, and everything was done all in good fun.

Next week I will be on vacation in Florida. I heard David and Keith talking about hiking another mountain while I am away. I hope they use wisdom as I will not be there to give them my experience and life-saving guidance.

And that, my friend, is winter hiking.

Merry Christmas to Me.

A nice six-mile round trip to the Pawtuckaway fire tower in the freezing rain. It doesn't get any better! I got incredibly sick.

A week later, another Pawtuckaway hike, this time to the fire tower. I didn't want to go because I was still feeling under the weather, but these two older guys needed a guide. One of whom was non-stop whining, "We're off-trail, I need to stop, my ice creepers are jammed up with snow..." SMH

Anyway, it was a beautiful, sunny day for a hike.

15 THE STORY OF MT. PASSACONAWAY

Passaconaway is an Indian word meaning, "make fat man cry like baby."

I plan on enjoying a wonderful week of vacation. You know where you sit around and do nothing, maybe watch some TV. But no, I get a call from my two buddies, Keith Tilton and **Dave Salois**, who say they would like to go hiking. After making plans and loading up the car at four in the morning, we headed off to the Great North.

We did the Dicey's Mill Trail. When we started hiking at sunrise, it was 7° below zero. It was so cold I didn't even have to walk, I started shivering so much I vibrated up the trail. By the time we summited, temps had heated up to a balmy five degrees.

Now Keith had run five miles a couple times that week and David had hiked Mt. Cannon the day before. Meanwhile, I had sat around for a month being overworked and sick. Most people don't know a little medical secret I've discovered: it's not the chicken soup, it's the pepperoni pizza that is great for healing, but not so much for hiking. Nothing beats comfort food when you're feeling down.

I would like to add that David skipped church to climb Mt. Cannon on a Sunday, but I'll come back to that later in the story. The trail was incredibly rugged because people had hiked it when the snow was melting which left lots of postholes. It then refroze and became impossible to navigate. We needed to cross a swollen river that was two feet deep and twelve feet wide and all we could find was a blowdown. At first, I was the only one brave enough to go across the twelve-inch diameter tree. The other guys were so amazed at my bravery that they took my picture as I forged my way across the blowdown. It's one of my favorites as it brings out my rugged side. Keith and David did finally work up the courage to cross on it as there were no other options. They both had great big grins like two kids who accomplished something they never thought they could do.

When you're 260 pounds and trying to cross a river on a small blowdown, you use a lot of muscles you never knew you had just trying to keep your balance. Sure, it may have taken me a little longer than expected to cross, but for Keith and David to be rolling around in the snow laughing as they watched me was a little uncalled for.

Again, on the way up and most of the way back, I was leading point. Remember, that is the position that needs the strongest and most experienced hiker. I was glad to do my part. (I had learned from frontier history that the point person had to be the best looking as well, so when a hostile tribe of Indians was encountered, the person's natural good looks would deescalate the situation. I can only imagine if my companions were in the lead and we met a lost, forgotten tribe. The arrows would have flown so thick we would never have made it back to the car before becoming pin cushions.)

At a little over ten miles, the hike started off with a steep incline that went on for mile after mile before getting into some switchbacks. The trail leveled off but soon turned into another very steep climb, almost vertical to the summit. We had to traverse some interesting ice floes as well. There were times on the way up when my legs felt like they were going to explode, and my breathing was so labored I thought I saw my lungs come out in front of me.

We finally summited and despite the frigid temps, got some great pictures as it was a beautiful, sunny day.

As we started our descent, I mentioned that Mt. Whiteface was only a mile away and we could double summit, but David and Keith said, "No!" Hiking is a no-judgment zone, so whatever one wants to do the others comply without griping or hazing... and so we started down.

A little further on, my legs started getting sore as the descent seemed endless. Then I started getting really, really hungry. I was in desperate need of more fuel but only had a lousy sawdust bar. David on the other hand had a salami sandwich that he didn't eat; I kept hinting about how hungry I was and how just one little bite would really satiate me. Just a nibble of sandwich would revive my strength and allow us to go on as a team. David, however, refused to be moved and never offered me his sandwich. That's why I mentioned earlier that he probably shouldn't skip church too often to go hiking because it is at church that he would learn about the Christian virtue of sharing. After all, "It's more blessed to give than to receive."

We finally got back to the car and were heading home. Every part of my body was hurting - and I was still hungry. I again mentioned the sandwich. In a casual, carefree tone, David said he had thrown it away. (Is there a stiffer jail sentence for committing bodily harm against a chief of police??)

During the ride, Keith mentioned he wanted to hike again on Friday. Total insanity! Not a hobby at all! More of a malady!

These mountains have ratings of easy, moderate, and difficult. The ratings mean nothing. Anything over 4,000 feet is difficult. As a matter of fact, they should be rated

1) difficult,

2) so difficult it's not worth the patch, and

3) insanely difficult and you should just stay in bed.

I can't wait to finish all forty-eight mountains, so I can get that dang patch and go back to living a normal life. In fact, I'm thinking of buying about 20 of them and sewing them on everything I can.

And that, my friend, is hiking.

Just did the South Mt. Fire Tower Trail at night with this motley crew. Six and a half miles in the snow using headlamps. Great hike but the Super Moon skunked us as it was socked in with clouds.

16 THE STORY OF MT. ROBERTS

Standing 2,600 feet in elevation, Mt. Roberts in Moultonborough is one of the '52 With a View'.

After getting over the flu and missing about five weeks of hiking, I had the great idea of calling my hiking buddy, Keith Tilton and saying, "Let's do Mt. Roberts. It is not that strenuous. Certainly not a 4,000 footer and it will be fun."

After an illness, it is wise to condition on a smaller mountain rather than chancing a poor performance on the bigger ones.

As we began our ascent, we realized that hiking in six inches of freshly fallen snow was like trying to walk up a sand dune or going up a down escalator. It reminded me of the little boy who had to explain why he was late to school. He told the teacher the snow was so slippery that for every two steps he took forward, he slid back three. She asked how he had made it there if that were true. He said, "I turned around to go home."

The snow-covered trail was pocketed with hundreds of post-holes made by previous hikers, making it incredibly difficult to find good footing. I'm sure in the summer this is a fun hike that I would hop up like a deer frolicking in the woods. But in these winter conditions, I found myself sucking air and physically holding my heart in my chest to keep it from coming right out. There were some great views up there, but we couldn't see them because the fog came in so thick I could have hiked with my mouth open and stayed hydrated.

We met some other hikers whose steps had helped pack the trail down for our descent; they were all smiles saying, "Isn't this great?" I never knew there were so many psychotic people in New Hampshire.

When we got back, I dropped Keith off and he made noises getting out of my car that I've never heard him make before. They certainly weren't noises of "Great hike, Pastor, can't wait to do it again." I don't know why I keep doing this to myself. I don't know if this whole Forty-eight Footer Club is worth it.

I stand above the forest, observed in plain view.

But what you cannot see of me, you cannot see of you.

Some eyes gazing upwards, fully satisfied.

Walk away contented, my trails never tried.

Yet others hear a challenge in my upward sweep,

and brave the path less traveled, to ascend the steep

Driven by the glory to see what I see.

Pushing past the struggle that's in you, not in me.

When you reach the pinnacle to behold what I behold

You find you did not conquer me, but what was in your soul.

I am a mountain!

Ken Bosse 2019

17 THE STORY OF MT. CABOT

Mt. Cabot is named after an Italian explorer. Mamma mia, I kid you not! Like, what did he discover, the bad piece of sausage on the pizza?

Seriously? A NH mountain named after him? SMH. Why not an early movie star like ZaSu Pitts? I think that would be a cool name for a mountain.

I knew this hike was going to have issues when one of my hiking buddies told me that before a hike, he cut his toenails to reduce the chance of toe pain. Well, I guess I got carried away when I clipped and saw blood. That came back to haunt me.

It had been a while since climbing a 4,000 footer, so I called my good hiking buddy, Keith Tilton, who said he was good to go. Tim Mailloux said he had to change the fluid in his headlights but after serious pressure he caved. David Salois had climbed it before, so he said he had to prepare a sermon, which I thought odd seeing as he's the Chief of Police. Anyway, that left the three of us to steal away at 5 a.m. Mt. Cabot is the farthest northern mountain of all forty-eight, so it took some time to get there. Oh, how I despise Rt. 16.

The dirt road in was solid ice and only expert driving on my part got us there. Oh sure, there was the occasional, "Look out!" and, "We're going to die!" but my skills prevailed. I was concerned if it warmed up and water formed on the ice, we'd never be able to leave. Good thing there were at least two strong hiking buddies available for pushing as I would skillfully steer.

When we started the hike, it was a balmy nine degrees.

As we started up the trail the mountain looked small in the background. Then it dawned on me that the mountain was three miles away.

The sign announced the route as the Kilkenny Trail. A prophetic name which is pronounced Kill Kenny. (That's me!)

You see, my problem is I have the muscle tone of Gumby (just aged myself there). I thought I was doing great when Keith (the 69-year-old) needed to rest from the pace I was setting. Then I found out it was because he ran four miles the day before, then walked another two miles. He absolutely amazes me.

The snowshoe enthusiasts had gone before us and made a nice little fourteen-inch wide path that if you stepped off it, you found yourself up to your waist in snow. Thank you, snowshoeing people. I couldn't have done it without you, because I wouldn't have done it without you. Don't get me wrong, I have two pairs of snowshoes and I wear them to prevent postholing when needed, but I'm not crazy about being the one who goes out and breaks trail after twelve inches of freshly fallen snow. Trail-breaking takes a special skill called being in shape. I once broke trail in Pawtuckaway through eight inches of fresh snow. After ¾ of a mile, I was a hot mess. I said there must be something else better to do today. I went home and had some spaghetti.

During the whole journey, we had to jump across streams that had steep banks on each side with a three to four-foot jump to keep from falling into open flowing water. No problem going up, but after nine miles round trip, coming down became very interesting. (I could jump the farthest... not bragging, just fact.)

By the time we summited, temps had dropped to zero degrees. The Mt. Cabot cabin is at the top and it was a welcome place to get out of the breeze. As my two companions ate and hydrated, my keen eye noticed the telltale signs of hypothermia setting in. Sluggish, slurred speech. No desire or energy to move. Stuffing food in their mouths. No longer talking, reduced to just grunting. I had to act fast in order to save their lives, so... I broke wind.

A lot!

I turned that little cabin into a house of horrors. It had its intended effect. Immediately they revived and started cursing and getting their gear on. I even noticed tears of thanks. For after all, I had just saved their lives. You're welcome! Hypothermia is a horrible way to go.

As we descended, it was hard to keep up with Tim as he was now running full steam down the mountain. Hikers are so funny the way they act sometimes. Totally unpredictable.

During our exit through the winter woods, I noticed no one was talking. I didn't mind because my nasal passages started feeling funny. Then I realized it was just my boogers that were freezing. I was going to announce it to the guys, but they seemed focused on making good time, so I let it go.

As we approached the road, we saw a sanding truck go by, and we were all thankful that no one would have to push the car. The ride home was awesome. My buddies just stared out the windows so taken in by the NH beauty that they didn't even speak.

Getting closer to home I heard one mutter, "Jerk!" Then the other reply, "Total jerk!"

I don't know what happened to make them mad at each other.

Totally unpredictable!

And that, my friend, is hiking.

The Story of Mt. Cabot Part 2

I know! I know what you're thinking. How can there be a part two?

Well, it all starts with my Suunto watch the church gave me for Pastor Appreciation Day.

That watch does everything but climb the mountain for you. One of its features is that it creates a video of your hike as a map on 3D topography. Wicked cool, wicked pissah… that is until later that week when I watched our climb of Mt. Cabot. I couldn't believe my eyes. We never summited. We missed it by two-tenths of a mile.

When I say we, I mean Keith Tilton and Tim Mailloux. How could they have missed that? Just beyond the hut is the dome rock where the old fire tower stood. Guess what? That's not the summit. I wish someone would put a yellow flashing light with a sign that says, "Not there yet, dummy".

Both of my pals said, "So what, we still hit 4,000 feet. Let it go."

But I couldn't. It haunted me for days, losing sleep, not being able to eat… well, losing sleep.

I just couldn't take credit for something I didn't do. So, I called all my good hiking buddies six days later to see who would hike it again with me. Tim said something about an impending alien invasion, but Keith was in and so was David.

I was glad that David was going because I knew he'd get me to the right summit location.

New friend, **Bret Hazelwood**, also said he would like to go but he wanted to bring his dog, Eli. No problem. We left at 5 a.m.

I had met Eli before, so it was fun seeing David and Keith meet this dog that weighed 165 pounds and looked like a grizzly. Hahaha! They turned whiter than a just-washed hospital sheet in the sun.

After arriving, we spiked up and headed out on our nine and a half mile quest. I had remembered the first attempt as being a fun, slow, easy hike but conditions had changed. Five inches of freshly fallen snow lightly tamped down by an early snowshoe hiker gave us just enough slip that made the hike unbearable. I mean not even the Navy Seals put their guys through what we went through. My hips felt like they were coming unhinged. I was just two heartbeats under cardiac arrest and breathing like a horse with whooping cough. I had never had issues with my hips, but they were letting me know they were there on this hike.

Every time I stopped to recover, I would turn and observe the grinning face of David who wasn't even sweating or breathing hard. And he had climbed Mt. Lafayette the day before. He's not human!!!

Brett said he loved my pace because he was really out of shape. Wait, what?

Why do I hike with these guys?

We finally made it to the infamous cabin and were enjoying some grub when Eli started passing gas. That dog has no couth.

We completed the two stinking tenths of a mile to the actual summit, all the time me cursing myself in my mind and Keith cursing me out loud.

Then my good buddies said, "Ken go over there for a pic." I walked slowly off the Snowshoe monorail and the next thing I knew, I had sunk up to my chest. The snow up there was unbelievable! I was panicking a little because I still hadn't touched bottom. The only thing holding me up from totally vanishing was my backpack. My pals were busy with their cameras and, only after they felt they had the perfect pic, did they help me out. So much fun!

The hike down was purely demonic. It had warmed up enough to cause the snow to become sticky and ball up under our spikes. So off they came. The only problem was the snow was also very slippery.

The way down was half hiking and half skiing.

I was flailing around and grabbing for trees because, when I started sliding, I would also start running and running down mountains isn't very wise.

Keith instructed me to sink in my heels and to do that I needed to goose-step like a Nazi paratrooper.

At the next steep section, I let Keith lead the way. One goose step, two goose steps, then slip and slide and that goose was taking flight.

I laughed my head off until I realized I was next. Each one of us did that trail like drunken figure skaters with vertigo.

My legs were so tired when we hit the last two miles of the flat hike that they threatened mutiny. They said they'd cut off the blood supply. I was too tired to argue.

We got to Bret's van and I said, "Keith, don't you feel better knowing you did it?" I won't repeat word for word, but his reply was in the negative.

On the ride home poor Eli slept like a log... as did David and Keith.

Later that night I slept like Eli to the point Darlene said I was barking in my sleep and howling.

And that, my friend, is hiking.

Here's a little add-on from my third trip (this time in summer) up Mt. Cabot to help Ian, who still needed to scratch it off his list.

As we were going up, we hear, "Excuse me!" This 20-something girl with her two dogs, came running up the trail. RUNNING! I know it's a thing but, dang!

Before we reached the summit, we hear, "Excuse me," and there she passes on her descent.

Ian and I are now descending and I'm sweating like a hippo running towards an ice cream mirage, "Excuse me," and here she comes again. I was speechless. I was blown away. I was as stupefied as a man with a lisp trying to say 'lisp'. A little further down trail… you guessed it, "Excuse me," sounded again in our ears. As she ran past, I asked, "Are we going to see you on a third trip?" She started laughing (how was she even breathing?) and said, "I'm doing a silly list. I'm trying to see if I can run each forty-eight twice in one day". I'm amazed at the human drive to push itself to the limit. I called out to her and said, "Good luck with Owl's Head," then I pushed myself to get to a restaurant to order a burger.

18 THE STORY OF MT. FLUME, PART 1

I know what you're thinking: Why is there a part one? Are you expecting a part two? Well, it's funny you should ask.

It was time to attempt another 4,000 footer, so I asked around and found out that only my good hiking buddy Keith Tilton and Bret Hazelwood were able to go. I knew Bret would be bringing his 165-pound mini grizzly bear dog along with him, which was fine with me because it's fun to watch people discover him on the trail. It's amazing how fast people can run in snowshoes.

We set off at our usual departure time which is when the sun is still shining on China and headed north for Mt. Flume. If you remember, in earlier stories when we were on Mt. Liberty and about a mile and a half from Mt. Flume, we had entertained the thought of completing a double summit. However, it was way too cold and icy that day, so we decided to wait for a different time. Also, you will remember in an earlier post, Keith and I climbed a much smaller mountain called Mt. Roberts in which we encountered just enough snowfall to make that trail pure hell. I remember making the comment that I sure wouldn't want to do a

4,000 footer in these conditions. Well, lo and behold, hell came home to roost. We started off with a half-inch of snow which, as we got higher, turned into an inch, then an inch and a half, then two inches; it eventually got deep enough to make it downright difficult, similar to hiking up a sand dune, except colder. The leg workout was like having them repeatedly beaten with baseball bats.

You would think by now that I would be getting in better condition. I honestly think I'm putting on more weight. I know there are some health nuts that think you should eat like a rabbit, but honestly, at 59 years old, what's left in life? I do believe in fitness! Like fittin' this whole cheeseburger in my mouth. And of course, I want Abs…solutely all the bacon to go on it as well.

I honestly do watch what I eat and have cut out soda and sweets. I eat a lot more salads and I have cut out most carbs, but it is still difficult. Nevertheless, I continue to lug the extra weight up a 4,000 foot mountain with a group of hiking buddies that could do it in half the time. I think the AMC should create a 'Fatty Patch' because it's twice as hard at 59 and 40 pounds overweight than at 20 years old and in your prime. I think a hiker with a big pot belly falling down a mountain to an awaiting ambulance would make a great patch.

I definitely qualify for the Fatty Patch.

Anyway, we made it to about 3,300 feet when we encountered the ladders. These are mounted on a rock that is so steep you can't continue without them. I'm not talking about the flimsy aluminum things you can get at the box store. These are trees that have been hewn down and built into a ladder that a grizzly could climb with pride. However, when we got to these ladders, we didn't realize they were there because they were buried beneath snow and ice. We thought the trail had just gotten ridiculously steep and we had to scramble up anyway. Keith and I did a 50 foot section and then turned around to look back at how far we had come. Bad move! Never look down! Brett, with all his youth, stamina and strength, was already going up higher and telling us it wasn't getting any better.

So, our age and wisdom decided to call it a day and turn around. Not only that, Keith had started crying and I was muttering like a crazy person. "I'll never see Darlene again; I'm going to die up here." The cold, along with pure fear, can play tricks on the human mind.

I do not regret that decision at all. It just means I'll have to go back in the summer and do that blankety-blank-blank-blank mountain again. Oh well, I had to do Mt. Cabot twice and I'll have to do Mt. Osceola again, so why not.

It was still a nine and a half-mile hike on a beautiful day up to 3,300 feet and even if we didn't summit, it beats a day at the office.

Winter hiking is tricky. It can also be dangerous. When in doubt, turn around. The mountains will always be there.

And that, my friend, is hiking.

Here's a thought…

You are so unique that your palm lines are unlike any other person. You are so unique that your fingerprints are like the barcodes on a package and the FBI can log multiple millions in a database. You are so unique that your eye scan is like an unbreakable combination to a safe. You are so unique that facial recognition software can pick you out of billions of people. You are so unique that every cell in your body is stamped with coded DNA. There is not now, never has been, or ever will be anyone like you. You are unique.

19 THE STORY OF MT. OSCEOLA & EAST PEAK

Mt. Osceola is the name of a native tribal Indian chief who was known for torturing old, overweight white men. He would make them climb these two mountains named after him, and most of those people never made it out of the woods again.

My story begins with winter hikes on smaller mountains in the Lakes Region of New Hampshire. That winter I logged in 20 peaks with my good buddy, Keith Tilton. At one point in time, I wanted to quit the torture of hiking in snow but a friend, Reanna Valley, encouraged me to keep on because as she said, "The conditioning would really show itself in the spring."

I picked up Keith at 6 a.m. and we headed for the great north after our routine stop at Dunkin's. When we got there, we were dismayed to find the road was still closed with a remaining two miles to the trailhead. Keith insisted that we just move the sawhorses and drive-in. I was concerned because I never do anything that's illegal, but Keith was adamant. In the long run, it was a good call because it saved us two miles one way from what was going to be an eight-mile in and out hike. Also, I knew that if I got a ticket of any kind, he would pay it because I had photo evidence of him moving the barriers. Hehehe!

We hit the trail and, much to my amazement, Reanna's words proved to be true. From the car to the summit of Mt. Osceola, we only stopped one time for two minutes while I put on my sweatband and took a sip to stay hydrated.

I was feeling like a new hiker. Okay, let's face it, at this time I thought I was the reincarnation of Grizzly Adams. We summited Mt. Osceola after encountering every trail condition imaginable from large boulders, to rocks, to wet rocks, to slab rocks, to mud and gravel, snow and ice, and standing water, and tons of blowdowns that made us crawl on our hands and knees. Do you know what everyone remembers about their military service? Bootcamp! This mountain should have been called Mt. Bootcamp!

The views at the top were stellar and a nice reward for the hard work. It was a beautifully clear day in the low eighties. Then my eyes glazed over to East Osceola and much to my amazement, I realized the maps lied as far as indicating that it was level from one peak to the other. It was more of a 500 foot drop down and a 300 foot ascent up incredibly steep trails. I truly believe that mapmakers have these sadistic laughing episodes every time they imagine someone looking at one of their maps and saying, "That doesn't look bad at all."

We had read in the trail description about a rock formation called The Chimney, a 27 foot vertical section of trail, I was anticipating it with trepidation because my bladder was full, and I had not yet addressed that problem.

As we were descending and the trail got steeper and steeper, it scared the daylights out of me. I mean, let's face it, of all the things I pack, I normally don't pack another pair of underwear. I warned Keith of the dangers of the steep rocks covered with loose gravel.

Keith making his way down the trail.

As we slowly made our way to the bottom, I said, "If that was not the chimney, we're in big trouble". Just then, we both glanced 50 feet to the left and saw the horrors of what is… The Chimney!

Good old Chief Osceola knew how to take care of old, unconditioned, white men.

I decided to put it out of my mind and push on to the summit of East Osceola. Push is an understatement as the trails became incredibly steep. My legs, which were once bounding with energy, were now beginning to get tired. Remember that tired is hiking logo for "I think my feet are falling off one toe at a time." My legs started quivering like sixteen-year-olds on their first date.

The summit of East Osceola wasn't even worth the picture. It was just a pile of rocks in the middle of the forest. I mean, really? Can't someone put up a hotdog stand or something?

We turned around and headed out. Then we came face-to-face with The Chimney. Without even thinking about what I was doing, I tackled it and started climbing upwards. It was like I had suddenly become Spiderman and there wasn't any cliff I could not scale. I don't know if it was fatigue or oxygen deprivation, but I attacked that thing like it had insulted my mother. I certainly earned my man card that day. Keith took a picture and then, with the ten years he has on me and all the wisdom those years have given him, quickly decided to go around to the alternate route.

About halfway up The Chimney, I encountered a three-foot area of rock that was protruding outwards. That, with a combination of my belly which also protrudes, caused a real problem. Hold the man card. Instead of panicking, I prayed, "Lord will you keep me safe?" The answer I believed I got was, "Yes, Darlene has prayed for your safety because she says she does not yet have the right amount of life insurance on you." Now I don't know if that was what was said, but I do remember reminding myself to have a conversation with Darlene that night. I made it to the top of The Chimney with a renewed belief in my ability to do what I set out to do and a whole bunch of new gray hairs. I also learned that from here on out I needed to pack more underwear.

Every time I encounter an obstacle like The Chimney, I foolishly think it must be the worst one there is. Now I don't want to discourage any new hikers but let me say that every hike prepared me for what the next hike would bring. Kind of like a blind date when you say, "It's got to get better after that....".

We summited Mt. Osceola, which I had already climbed before by the way. It is just that I had to go over it once again to reach East

Osceola or face a slide trail that some people think is fun. Slide trails are nothing more than avalanches that people hike up. Nay, nay, not for me! Around this time, we started our 3.2 miles descent back to the car. My legs were getting used up. That means at this point, they were basically like two pool noodles, unresponsive and no strength left. I have found that on the descent it's easier to hop on the tops of the rocks rather than trying to step around them. The only danger comes if you slip on a rock and your legs are in a weakened state. You are going to have a phenomenally bad fall. Your hiking buddies will quickly take out their cameras and take pictures to post on their Facebook pages. None the less, I hopped the rocks.

When we got back to the car, I told Keith that my legs were a little tired. Again, that's hiking jargon for "I don't think I can take another ten steps without falling flat on my face." We started driving back, and I stopped at a Dunkin's to rehydrate. That frozen mocha drink ministered to my very soul. Oh, my goodness, it was yummy.

When I got home, I went to get out of my car and there was a little twinge of pain in my legs. Interpretation: my legs screamed at me, "Oh my God, what are you doing to us and, whatever it is, don't ever do it again." Nonetheless, within five minutes I was bouncing up and down the stairs at my house. My legs had totally recuperated, and I was already thinking about the next hike. I think it might be Mt. Flume.

And that, my friend, is hiking.

20 THE STORY OF MT. FLUME... AGAIN

This was my third look at Mt. Flume. The first one was when we summited Mt. Liberty in winter conditions and Mt. Flume was a mile away. But it was way too cold that day to add another summit and two extra miles to our trip.

This brings up an important warning in hiking: When to Turn Back.

My first preference is to turn back as soon as I am physically spent, but there are no summits a half-mile from the parking lot.

My second preference is to turn back when my food is gone, and I'm getting hungry. But again, the half-mile thing.

Seriously, you need to be honest about the red flags that surround your comfort zone and physical condition and know when to call it a day. As someone once said, "The mountains will always be there."

Knowing the forecast and reading weather conditions are extremely important in the Whites. Things change fast and it doesn't take long to get caught off guard. When in doubt, bailout. No one planned a hike with the goal of needing to be rescued or, even worse, dying. Know your limits, heed the red flags, respect how quickly the weather can change and never, ever feel ashamed for turning around. EVER! This book is dedicated to the incredible men and women of NH Search and Rescue and I believe they would all agree with my caution.

The second attempt for Mt. Flume was another winter hike. At that time the snow and ice were so deep that the ladders were not accessible and the steepness of the mountain at that point was too dangerous without proper traction, such as crampons and an ice ax, ropes, harness, Sherpas and a musk ox. Not sure why I'd need a musk ox, but it sounds cool. The telltale signs of difficulty were all around. Namely, the monorails that snowshoes make stopped at the ladders. Even then, we courageously tried to push on another 50 feet of elevation only to look down. Never look down! I didn't remember the snow being yellow on the way up…

Now came part three. It was in late spring when I called my good hiking buddy, Keith Tilton, and said, "Let's try Mt. Flume again." After a long while, he groaned and moaned and said, "Would you quit crying? I'll go already." We loaded into the car at 6 a.m. and headed for the great north.

I believe Flume is an Indian word meaning death. It is where the writer of the *Lord of the Rings* got the idea for Mount Doom. Just another way of saying Mt. Flume.

On the ascent, I discovered something new about summer hiking. I call them the hordes of hell, but most people know them as black flies. I don't know what is worse, having them bite you or inhaling one because your breathing is sucking in more than a black hole. You can cough all you want, that sucker isn't coming out. Oh, gotta love hiking. I've seen grown men hack and cough and dry heave trying to dislodge a black fly, only to admit defeat with a gulp of water followed by the downward stare of humiliation.

I made three crucial mistakes on this hike:

Number One: I had been wrestling with insomnia all week long and the night before the hike I only got about four hours of sleep. That would come back to haunt me.

Number Two: I did not eat breakfast. Combined with not hydrating properly, that led to having dizzy spells and being unable to focus as we got closer to the summit. Some of that may have been from the never-ending prattle of Keith's stories, but it was still quite alarming. I was thinking... "Well, these conditions should make the descent pretty interesting." Some food from my backpack and a little bit of Gatorade put me right back on track.

Number Three: I was wearing the wrong kind of socks and about mile seven they started acting like sandpaper. My feet felt like a couple of tenderloins with the accent on tender.

After hiking for what seemed like an eternity, we encountered all the ladder systems that had been buried in snow on our last attempt.

This was an eleven-mile round trip hike that felt like taking a gentle stroll to NY. OMG!!!

On my way up, my weakened condition made me feel like I was climbing Mt. Denali. I was using all my focus to just keep putting one foot in front of the other. I could even hear background music in my mind that overdramatized the feeling. Of course, I've learned by now to ignore Keith's yawning as he feels the pace is a little too slow. It is hysterically funny because last week when we climbed Mt. Osceola, I went from the car to the summit with only a two minute stop. On this hike, I was stopping quite a bit because I was having a hard time recovering. My heart felt like it had just eaten pop rocks. I was sweating profusely and the veins on my forehead made me look like an angry Klingon. "You just got to eat breakfast." Let me restate that, "I just have to eat breakfast".

The summit was extremely gnarly but also very photogenic. The reward of busting out of the tree line onto a rocky summit on a beautiful sunny day really can't be put into words. Mostly because I'm breathing so hard that my mind and lips can't form any.

On the way down, my feet were killing me, but I had to keep going. Push past the pain. Of course, I only mentioned to Keith that my legs were tired. If you remember hiking jargon, that means that I'm in so much pain that my legs will be in traction for at least a month before I'll ever stand on them again.

All in all, it is still another forty-eight 4K footer that is completed, and we had a lot of fun in beautiful weather conditions. The views were stunning. From this point on, the trails will get longer and steeper and some will have multiple summits. I question why I keep doing this. I thought bucket lists were things you wanted to do before you died, not things you do that kill you in the process.

And that, my friend, is hiking.

21 THE STORY OF MT. ISOLATION

Shortly after the creation of the White Mountains, some angels questioned God about why He created a four thousand foot mountain and placed it out in the middle of nowhere all by itself. The Lord responded by saying, "In time you will see why, and we will have a hysterical laugh about it..." *(to be continued)*

There is something about hiking the New Hampshire woods. There is a rugged quality in the hardwoods mixed with softwoods and the up and down rolling features of the landscape. Everywhere you look you find granite boulders left by some ancient glacier. New Hampshire is called the Granite State for good reason: the boulders and blowdowns get covered in moss and lichens that create a mystical feel to the forest. There's something wild here. Wild, yet peaceful. On some days there's a fog or mist that closes you in with your immediate surroundings and you feel like you've been whisked away in time to a place that is only experienced by an invitation from the forest itself. It's a good kind of addiction.

However, when you think of the word isolation, what comes to mind? Being alone? Solitary confinement? A place so forbidding that people slowly stare into the abyss and go mad, becoming mumbling, drooling psychopaths? That pretty much sums up this mountain.

My hiking buddy, Dave Salois, is part Micmac Indian. In his native tongue, the mountain was called "yougottabekiddingme". Translated in English, it is Mt. Isolation. It was used to banish Micmac Indians who caused trouble and told bad jokes. Indians who went there were never heard of again. They probably drowned somewhere on the Rocky Branch Trail. Yup, that's right... drowned.

The weather for this Spring day looked great and I called my good hiking buddy, Keith Tilton, and said, "Hey how about we hike Mount Isolation?" After consulting the maps, we realized this twelve-mile hike would be a full day's work. I picked him up at 4:30

a.m. That's right, 4:30 a.m. on my day off! Part of mountain hiking consists of being intermittently insane. If you have that down, the rest comes easy. Darlene had gotten up really early and made us a couple of breakfast sandwiches and Keith had brought some raspberry squares. After a quick stop at Dunkin's for some coffee, we were all set and headed up to the great north.

Because the hike was going to be a lot longer than usual, I brought four liters of water rather than my usual two. When placed just the right way in a well-constructed backpack, the weight is dispersed so that it only feels like one or two tons. We exited the car and immediately the trail went up and up and up. Within a mile and a half, we were registering 2,050 feet on my altimeter. The trail then descended ever so slightly for the next two miles; this would become a huge problem on the way out when I'd be walking on legs of spaghetti. This is the time the Lord called the angels around Him for a good laugh. The snickering had started. The trail conditions were designed and manufactured by Lucifer himself. Almost all the trail was covered by standing water or deep mud with rocks scattered throughout. It wasn't exactly hiking as much as rock hopping. Hiking can be fun. Rock hopping is one of the most grueling exercises I've ever been through. By this time the angels were popping popcorn and enjoying some good belly laughs. My heart rate was somewhere between 120 and the speed of hummingbird wings.

Let me put it this way, the conditions were so bad that even Keith Tilton, who calls me the big whiner, was getting into a little bit of the whining act.

A lot of people ask what's the best way to get conditioned for hiking. The generic answer is "hike". While that is very true, I would recommend starting on flat hikes and gradually moving up to smaller mountains such as the ones in Pawtuckaway State Park or the Belknap Range. Deep knee bends can't hurt, but my favorite is eating pizza while watching movies about hiking.

Back to Mt. Isolation… If the trails weren't bad enough, there was the stream or, should I say the river, that we had to cross five times. Whoever made this trail must have been out of their minds! Why cross the river five times? Keith fell in on an attempted river crossing and scuffed up his knee but was no worse for wear. Nothing a Batman band-aid could not make better. I have gotten used to the sight of blood as I usually somehow end up bleeding on every mountain. "Can't fool the mountains, Pilgrim, the mountains have a way of their own," (Jeremiah Johnson). We pushed on through more elevation and, when the trail finally turned into a nice gravel path, we ran into a crazy number of blowdowns. It looked like a giant mess of pick-up sticks. This trail was impossible to hike at any kind of respectable speed as we were to find out nine and a half hours later. By now, the angels were rolling on the floor wiping tears from their eyes.

As we continued our approach, I noticed an incredible number of toads and it reminded me of Darlene's nickname for me. She got it from a British book where the main character is called Toad, a loveable, well-behaved, fun character. Yeah, that's me alright!

For lunch I had packed a salami and cheese sandwich in memory of David Salois who couldn't be with us. That sandwich really hit the spot. I held on to that memory because it would become the only good one of the day. David really knows what he's talking about when it comes to food. Salami and cheese have now become my all-time favorite sandwich.

At the summit we were swamped by an ungodly number of flies. I have no idea why they hang out on the top of 4,000 footers. I think it has something to do with Beelzebub, the Lord of the Flies. I guess I'll have to add a fly-swatter to my list of what to pack. After capturing a bunch of pics under a sunny sky, we started heading out. The smiles that the views had evoked soon vanished as we headed back into the dead man's march. Seven miles on tired legs began to take its toll. Someone had asked me if we ever see wildlife on our hikes. With all the moaning, groaning and whining sounds Keith was making, we wouldn't have even seen a deaf squirrel.

Going back through the swamps littered with rocks and the trails covered in water, stones and boulders were the only means of staying dry and my legs began to get tired. You will remember that's hiking jargon for "my legs have actively turned into fainting teenage girls at a Beatles' concert." (Told you I was old.)

I was dehydrating and drinking my remaining water at breathtaking speed.

We were beginning our final descent and both of us were running on sheer adrenaline. Just then I looked at the recorded distance on my watch and it read that we still had two miles to go. I cried. Keith cried. The deaf squirrel cried. I don't know how we finished. There was very little talking going on. I'm pretty sure it was at this time that the Lord dispatched a couple of his angels to help Keith along his way.

All kidding aside, we were both pretty ragged. Just then my car came into view, I sobbed as our hopes began to rise. This is the time in hiking where a voice from within starts shouting… "I'm going to make it! I'm actually going to make it!"

By far this was the most grueling hike I have been on to date, fourteen plus miles. I know in the future I will be faced with a couple hikes that will be eighteen miles or more, but now I'm thinking I might camp out, and make it a two-day hike. On the way home, we stopped at Dunkin's where I purchased a Watermelon Coolatta which hydrated my body and put my mind right.

The angels were rejoicing. Keith and I were laughing about the fact that David had not yet hiked this mountain. I can't wait until he does.

Misery loves company.

And that, my friend, is hiking.

The views make the odyssey worth it.

22 THE STORY OF MT. WHITEFACE

After doing the fourteen and a half-mile hike to Mt. Isolation and encountering the most horrible trail conditions in the world, you think I would have learned my lesson. Who forged the Rocky Branch trail anyway? A beaver? Half the dang thing is under water. But noooooo, I couldn't even wait a full week and I had to go hiking again. This is an indicator that the sickness has begun. Hikeitis is a very serious condition that has ruined marriages and bankrupted many an unsuspecting person. It's an addiction of the worst kind. Very few ever walk away from it. (Walk away from? Walk... see, it's everywhere.)

I contacted all my hiking buddies and even a couple of guys that I haven't hiked with, even a stranger I saw with a "will work for food" sign, and they all had excuses on why they couldn't go. They just made girly sounds and said, "Sorry." So, I just decided that this would be my first solo hike. In hindsight that may not have been the best idea, again, kind of like the frying the bacon in the nude thing.

I went to bed early, but I couldn't sleep. The thought of soloing was working on my imagination. I dreamed of bears, falls, broken bones and alien abductions. I woke up at 4 a.m. after about five hours of sleep and hit the road heading for the great north. The drive was lonely. I'm kind of a people person. I've discovered while hiking that there are your do-it-aloners and your groups of non-stop talkers and your, two-to-a-team hikers. I prefer to hike in groups of 20. That way I won't have to bother SAR when I fall and get a boo-boo. I've also noticed that there are the "don't talk to me" folks and the "friendlies" that love to stop and chat. It's a great community that reinforces the idea it takes all kinds to make the world go around.

In my last story, somebody had asked me if I ever see wildlife and I said, "No. Never." On this trip however, a deer walked out in front of my car, followed by a few turkeys and then a little later, a bunny rabbit. About a mile from the parking lot to the trailhead, a black bear was right in the road. If you had gotten a look in his eyes as I did, you would have seen he knew I was going to be hiking the Blueberry Trail and was moving fast to get there ahead of me. Why did I have to see a bear on my first solo hike? Notably, it is the only bear I have ever seen in the New Hampshire wilds. That fueled my imagination like gas to a 60's bra-burning party.

Anyway, after gearing up, I headed up the trail which was a nice walk through the woods and for about the first mile, I was looking in every direction with wide eyes while whistling a nice bear alerting song. I then encountered about a half-mile of slab rock that got a little steeper, followed by some real steep areas for a quarter of a mile or so, then back to a nice flat before it would get steep again. So far, it was turning into a glorious hike with Yogi nowhere in sight.

Then the trail got "really" steep. I mean like an elevator shaft without the elevator. I pushed on and was surprised to overtake three other hikers; this was a first, and I did it with great satisfaction and some disbelief. Notice I pass people when I'm alone. Just saying. Darlene had asked me how old the hikers I passed were and I told her that was none of her business. I passed them, that is all that matters. The trail leveled off again and lulled me into complacency and a false sense of security like a dentist saying, "You'll hardly feel a thing."

There are three minor summits on the way to the top, so I'd hit a steep part of the trail, then a summit, then a flat trail and on and on it went.

Then the fun began. Technical rock formations that looked like they belonged on the Dawn Wall of El Capitan. In some areas, the slab rock was so steep that it was kind of frightening. I'm glad my Columbia nylon pants dry quickly, if you know what I mean. A young guy with his German shepherd caught up to me right at one of the most horrible places. As the dog started to scramble the rock, it stopped and got a look in his eyes that seemed to say, "What the *%$#&."

And then, the wise animal turned and started heading back down the trail. The guy put his leash on the dog, but by this time I had passed them and inched my way around and up the crazy rock formation. I think that's all the dog needed. He seemed to think if that old, fat guy can do it, then I can do it. The next thing I knew, they were passing me again.

Now, when I say steep, I mean that this was hand-over-hand rock climbing. The problem with rock climbing is that the opposite is rock falling and that did not appeal to me as I was getting up to around 3,900 feet. Darlene would not have been impressed to see the dangerous conditions on this hike. At least not before taking out more life insurance on me. John Muir once said, "Of all the paths you take in life, make sure a few of them are dirt." He never hiked

Mt. Whiteface. No dirt, all rock. I must have gone over five or six of the gnarliest rock formations I've ever seen, all the time thinking I've got to go back down these suckers. I didn't get pics because I was by myself and after you reach one of these spots, it wasn't the time to stop for a Kodak moment.

I arrived at the summit, took some pics, drank some fluids, killed a million black flies, and then started back down. I was swinging at those flies like a Kung Foo master fighting a ghost.

I must admit there were times that I probably didn't look too gracious as I was sliding down slab rock on my butt. However, it's better to be safe than sorry. Some people were caught off guard by the sight of me sliding downhill, thinking I was a rockslide headed right for them. Did I ever mention I am six foot three and a tad overweight?

By this time, I had no more strength in my legs and the previous hiker had caught up to me. I should have been making really good time, but I was barely putting one foot in front of the other. You could have taken a still picture of me with a video camera. My tiring legs were reminding me I am really out of shape.

I finally made it down and was amazed to find the parking lot jam packed with cars. I got in my car and headed home. I was hot, tired, dehydrated, bitten by black flies, walking on legs that felt like mush and had a headache from too much direct sunlight.

I vowed that mountain twenty-four would be good enough. That's the halfway point of the forty-eight and seemed like a good quitting place for me.

I met a real lot of nice hikers on this trip and they fell into two groups. Either they were young and moving like the wind or they were old and sucking air like a dying walrus.

I was in the second category. I tell you, I'm done already. If you have never slumped into your car, covered in sweat, with barely the energy to drive home, you are not doing it right!

Enough is enough.

I wonder if David is off next Saturday?

And that, my friend, is hiking.

23 THE STORY OF MT. MORIAH

Moriah is a Hebrew name meaning "teacher." Oh boy, did I learn a lot! The first thing I learned is the psycho that rated this climb as "easy" should have his eye jabbed with a stick. What was he thinking? Listen, when you are 60 years old and 50 pounds overweight, there is no 4,000 foot mountain that's easy. Nuff said! I really don't think it's fair to have 20 or 30-year-olds who are Spartan runners and Marathon runners rate the difficulties of these mountains. It's cruel.

Someone once said, "We don't conquer mountains. We conquer ourselves." More like we kill ourselves.

I had a major brain cramp called "Forgetfulness". You ladies understand this the day after childbirth. You just successfully pushed a Buick out of your body while threatening your husband with bodily harm for looking at you with a twinkle in his eye. Four months later you're saying, "I think I'd like another baby." FORGETFULNESS!!!

After watching my legs turn into fluffernutters and getting blisters on my blisters and then saying within six days say, "I'd love to do that again." What? Really? Forgetfulness. At 4:20 a.m., I hit the road to pick up my hiking buddy, Keith Tilton, and arranged to meet an old friend who attended our church as a kid, Ian Kenney.

Mt. Moriah is part of the Carter-Moriah Ridge and runs along the northeastern side of Pinkham Notch. It stands at 4,049 feet and offers some awesome views. It was turning out to be a great day, 74 degrees with no humidity. The hike was nine miles and we encountered the steepest slab rock I've ever seen: 40° pitch on solid slab rock. Lots of it.

Here is part of my problem. I had bought a pair of hard-soled hiking boots. The issue with hard soles is they don't tend to grip well on rock and can lead to some slipping issues. I don't know if you have ever experienced what is called the "one-inch death", but it occurs when you slip just enough to watch your life pass before your eyes. Your heart stops, your bladder doesn't, you smack your knee, and adrenaline makes every step after that seem like walking through a minefield. These boots were so bad they gave me a panic attack whenever I saw slab rock. Mt. Moriah is nothing but slab rock. Steep slab rock!

I don't want to complain but did the pioneers that forged these trails literally look for the most forbearing parts and say, "Hold my beer, I got this." I'm pretty sure the trail could have zigged and zagged and missed half the crap I went up.

Here's a neat little hiking tip I'll let you in on. Learn how to ask open-ended questions in four or five words that will cause your hiking buddies to give long answers. Here's a good question, "So tell me, what was the most interesting date you've ever been on and why?" This allows you to breathe while pretending to be interested in their private lives. I am always trying to find ways to slow my hiking partners down because every one of them is faster than I am. Come to think of it, sloths move faster than I do. I came across this quote from John Muir; "Hiking - I don't like either the word or the thing. People ought to saunter in the mountains - not 'hike'! Do you know the origin of that word saunter? It's a beautiful word. Away back in the Middle Ages people used to go on pilgrimages to the Holy Land. When people in the villages through which they passed asked where they were going, they would reply, "A la sainte terre' (to the Holy Land). Thus, they became known as sainte-terre-ers or saunterers. Now these mountains are our holy land, and we ought to saunter through them reverently, not 'hike' through them."

What awesome words! Never truer than when you're the slow one.

When my hiking buddies start getting grumpy over the pace, I remind them; "I'm sauntering." Anyway, after sucking for air like a man seeing the ghost of his ex-wife, we finally made the summit, marshmallow legs and all. Great views are Mother Nature's way to trick me into believing that what I just went through was worth it. What would be worth it is if there was a Pizza Hut at the top.

After soaking in the sun and taking some pics, all good things must come to an end. The problem was, on the way down, it was so steep that my boots kept trying to push my toes out the backside of my heels. OMW. We saw two guys hiking barefoot. What the heck were they smoking on the ride north? WHY would they do that? Do they want their feet to look like a catcher's mitt?

If you are thinking of taking up hiking, let me remind you that there are other hobbies, such as Egyptian basket weaving or watching TV. If you're one of these people that hike traverses for 30 hours, get help!

Seriously, hiking is a very enjoyable hobby and I would en-courage anyone at any age or condition to give it a try. Remember to start slow. Walking the ice cream aisle at the supermarket is a great place to start. From there you can advance to one or two flights of stairs to a pub and then on to some trails. I really hope that reading about a 60-year-old fat man will encourage you, if I can do it, anyone can. "If I can do it?"

Ian

Here's a good tip. If you can't afford a helicopter to come and get you off the summit, make sure the soles of your boots have good grip on slab rock. I later purchased a pair of LL Bean Mount Katahdin Knife Edge boots. The grip was so amazing, I looked forward to encountering slab rock. What a difference the right boot makes.

After I arrived home, I discovered we had no power due to an outage and had to sit in my grime before I could take a hot shower. That was a miserable and uncomfortable two hours.

As I mentioned before, David Salois always encourages my hiking by reminding me that we see views that less than 1% of the people ever see. Riiiiiiight! And we feel the pain that only 1% are dumb enough to feel. I tell you, I think I'm done. This was number 25. I officially entered the last half. One over 50%. Good enough.

Come to think of it, I wonder what David is doing next week?

And that, my friend, is forgetfulness.

24 THE STORY OF THE TRIPYRAMIDS

I was looking forward to getting in one more of the 48 before heading out to California to backpack with my son Tim. I contacted my good buddy Keith Tilton and said, "Hey how about doing the Tripyramids?" Why settle for one when you can knock off two. Keith stuttered and stammered out something about being retired and resting. No one else from the crew was available to hike so Keith felt sorry for me and we headed off at 5 a.m. to the great north. There may have been a slight guilt trip about me falling, suffering, and dying all alone because he would not go.

Old friend, classmate and distant relative Glenn Lajoie, who had done the 48 when he was wiser and younger, told me, "Ken, wait till you do the Tripyramids." As if it was something exciting to look forward to. Come to think of it I never really liked that guy.

Are you kidding me, put together the word tri (there are three of them, although only two count as forty-eight 4,000 footers in New Hampshire), then add the word pyramid, which conjures up pictures of a structure so steep no one could ever scale it. Starting to get the picture? The pyramids of Egypt were built by space aliens who could levitate. That is why they are so steep. The trails up these mountains were built by space alien mountain goats.

Honestly, what human ever charted out this hike?

Keith and I hit the Sabbaday Brook Trailhead about 7 a.m. and found the first four miles a beautiful, somewhat flat, trail. However, the trail did cross the river seven times one way. SEVEN! That is a total of fourteen crossings round trip.

Both Keith and I experienced the one-foot plunge. Not too bad after fourteen crossings. I later learned the trail was first developed by local Indians who used it as a hunting and fishing trail. Why would they cross the river seven times? They must have been Micmacs. Dave Salois is part Micmac and it sounds like something he would do.

Hiking tip: River crossings. Don't do it! I know, I know. There are some rivers that just can't be avoided. Here is what you need to know to ensure your hike does not turn into a snorkeling adventure:

1) You're going to get wet.
2) Wet rocks are slippery.
3) Learning to hop rocks is a science that takes years to develop.
4) You're going to get wet.
5) Always let your friends go first, then follow the one that doesn't fall in.
6) If it is early spring and the winter runoff is so bad you cannot

see any rocks or hear your friends screaming to you over the noise of the river, turn around, go home, and watch TV.

7) You're probably going to get wet.

8) Always use your hiking poles to help keep your balance.

9) If you happen to make it across and do not fall in, don't get too cocky because you will have to come back and cross it again.

10) You're going to get wet.

11) If a river is on the list for a planned hike, bring an extra pair of socks and a life jacket because...

Keith gets it done!

Eventually the trail began to go up. At around 3,000 feet, it went straight up. I mean hand over fist rock climbing. Even Keith said he could not understand why they did not build ladders at such a steep area. Then he said he thought he was growing hooves and turning into a mountain goat. I wished I had hooves because I was scared to death. I had to put aside that it was Friday the 13th and trust in a greater power to get us to the top of this mountain. In other words, I was screaming, "Dear God help us!"

We finally made it to where the trail splits between the summits. First, we went right to North Tripyramid. The sparse views were no reward for the struggle of the hike. Then we headed back and took the left trail to Middle Tripyramid. This time the views were much better. We got the usual celebratory pictures and rested.

After grabbing some grub and hydrating, we headed back down. The 1,200 feet of nearly straight down trail took my breath away which was amazing seeing as how I was panting like a bull charging an elusive matador. It also made my heart pound as hard as it did while going up, but this time it was from fear rather than exertion.

Hiking tip: There is much debate in the hiking community about trail etiquette regarding who yields to whom? Do hikers descending yield to hikers ascending or do hikers ascending yield to hikers descending? The correct answer is - people going down should yield to hikers going up.

I don't know if that rings true on the Hancocks or Tripyramids after a dusting of snow. Seems it is easier going up versus trying not to slip and fall a thousand feet when going down. Therefore, in these kinds of conditions, those going up should not only defer but prepare to catch and stop someone coming down like an avalanche. Also, a little encouragement given to the descending person by pointing out trees to cling onto for dear life would be helpful. It is not easy spotting the hazards on the trail while crying from horror like a teenager who just walked in on his mom and dad in bed.

I found stopping for the groups of 30 foreign college students is wise no matter what direction they are heading. It also gives you a chance to check out the newest designer sneakers.

I have also realized that whether I'm going up or down, most people yield to me. I think it is because they hear my breathing and figure it's a medical emergency.

On our way out, little black flies swarmed around us. Not the kind that are lethal and biting, just those that hang out in your face to drive you crazy. Well, when you're huffing and puffing and sucking in air like a 747 jet engine, you know what inevitably happens. Yep, that is the second time I sucked one of those little guys in. You can hack and cough and spit all you want but they are too far back in your throat to dislodge them. Anyway, I guess it is protein and all part of the experience called hiking. This now makes number 27 of the forty-eight peaks I need to finish.

We made it back to the flat section of trail and eventually back to the car. We survived! As we were leaving, we met an elderly couple from Canada who were heading in. You could tell that they did not have a clue or the proper gear. They said they got lost and couldn't find the trail. That is probably the most fortunate thing that happened to them that day. If stupidity was a disability, more people would have handicap plates. I honestly don't know why there is not at least one fatality a week in the New Hampshire White Mountains. Some of the trails are that crazy.

"Then why do you hike them?" someone sane may ask. That is a great question isn't it? I'll let you know after my handicap plates come in!

And that, my friend, is hiking.

25 THE STORY OF NORTH & SOUTH KINSMAN

The two 4,000 foot mountains known as the Kinsman's North and South were named after Nathan Kinsman. On May 19, 1774, Nathan was appointed 4th Sargent, 1st Company, of the NH Militia. Nate was actually a veteran of the War of Independence. Way to go!

I found that hiking these mountains was a battle of its own and I'm not sure who won.

North Kinsman is 4,293 feet, while South Kinsman is 4,358 feet. The problem is that after climbing North Kinsman you descend back down to 4,000 feet and get to enjoy going up 358 more feet to the next summit.

Hiking buddy, David Salois, said that this trail was "epic". What he did not explain is that it is an acronym for "Emergency Personnel Immediately Called." I will also add that David graciously declined hiking with us as he has done all summer long. Hmmm?

After taking many long weeks off because of either hot or wet weather, I called my good hiking buddy, Keith Tilton, and said,

"Let's do a hike." I extended the invitation to another guy named Tom Bryant who is also, like Keith, retired. Tom has hiked some in the past. We set off at 5 a.m. and headed for the great north. I should have known things were not going to go well when the Dunkin's was closed.

We made it to the Mt. Lafayette Campground, put on our backpacks and headed out. After 1.8 miles, we made it to Lonesome Lake, an absolutely gorgeous and picturesque spot, well worth the hike. There are beautiful views of the lake with Mt. Lafayette in the background. We continued our trek upwards on the Fishing Jimmy Trail. This trail threw everything at us from gravel, rocks, boulders, waterfalls, streams, mud, more mud, log steps, ladders, slab rock, wet slippery slab rock, 6x6 inch wooden steps staked into rock, iron steps and even steps chiseled into the rock. It was absolutely nuts! This trail is rated as "difficult". If I gave it a rating, I would have thrown in a lot more adjectives.

I don't know who Jimmy was or what the heck he was fishing for, but no fish is worth it.

During the writing of this book, I was curious to know who Fishing Jimmy was. I found an excellent story written by Annie Trumbell Slosson called "Fishing Jimmy." You can find it on WikiSource. It tells the tale of James Whitcher from Franconia Valley. It is an amazing story. Turns out Jimmy found someone who loved fishing as much as he did.

I have since found out that my "friends" who had already hiked this went up a more sensible trail but never thought about sharing their knowledge.

This is a good place for another hiker's tip: Be kind and help folks who are new to hiking. If you discourage them too soon, they'll give up. Let them get bit by the hiking disease, then it's too late to avoid the hardships that lay ahead.

After going up for what seemed like forever, we stopped and saw the summit looming over us like the Grim Reaper himself with his sickle in his hand. That's when Tom in his age and wisdom said, "I'm going back to the hut." Had I known what lay ahead, I would have gladly joined him but, in my naivety, I pushed on to the summit just so I could gladly check them off my list of 4,000 footers.

We finally made the two summits only to realize that it was hazy, and the views were not very clear. Situation normal for another hike with Keith Tilton. I think he attracts clouds. We started heading down and that's when it started hitting me... I was out of juice. Batteries drained, completely dead, no more strength with four and a half more miles to go, all down incredibly steep paths.

This trail was tough! I wish conditioning would eventually make it easier to hike these trails, but that does not seem to be happening.

Poor Tom was back at the AMC Hut by Lonesome Lake waiting with a dead phone. We had told him it would only take us three hours, and we were already working on five. You know me, I wasn't about to start complaining, but Keith already had big tears rolling down his cheeks and I wanted to be optimistic.

Keith started getting so many charley horses, I thought he was going to open up some stables. It had become really humid and we had already finished all the water we had, still the trail went down. Dehydration is a funny thing. You really don't know what it's doing to you until it's too late. My legs felt like they were going to fall off and I was kind of wishing they would. My thighs hurt, my quads hurt, my knees hurt, and my kneecaps felt like that they were going to launch right off my knees. My calves hurt, my ankles hurt, my feet hurt, my toes hurt, even my toenails were hurting. Heck, even my hair hurt!

This trail made me consider the value of continuing in my quest to do all forty-eight. Why? Why? Why?

For a dang patch that says I did them, that's why.

When we finally made it back down to the hut, we looked like a couple of crazed loonies. My left eye kept winking while my head twitched to the right. Keith was shaking and both his feet had turned inward. Our breathing was labored and our eyes were sunken in. We both had four days of beard growth, yet we were clean-shaven at the start of the hike. We were overjoyed to find the hut had free, cold, fresh water. I made any camel proud and Keith drank twice as much as I did. Tom had a big grin on his face as if to say, "Haha! Suckers!" We hoisted our backpacks after having some snacks and headed back down the 1.8 miles to the car. I was never so glad to see my car. We turned the AC to 20 below zero and headed home.

Today, as I'm sitting here writing out my story, I am torn between selling my gear and never hiking again or plotting out the trail to Mt. Carrigan.

And that, my friend, is hiking!

"Come to the woods, for here is rest.
There is no repose like that of the green deep woods."
-- *John Muir*

26 THE STORY OF
NORTH & SOUTH TWIN MOUNTAINS

The Twins are named after Cain and Abel. One's nice. The other one will kill you. The mountains are rated as moderate.

Remember the ratings? Easy, moderate and difficult.

OK! Eating pizza is easy. Eating tacos is moderate. Eating baked beans with your fingers is difficult. These mountains were insane!

Getting up at 4 a.m. - difficult. Putting on a 20-pound pack - difficult. Hiking two and a half miles straight up - difficult. Listening to David Salois all day long - extremely difficult.

Weather wise, the day was promising to be a perfect hiking day. My good hiking buddy, Keith Tilton, said Hazel (his absolute angel of a wife) wouldn't let him go. Truth be told . . . he bought a motel room on wheels and was going camping. (Or should I say "recovering" from the Kinsman's we had done seven days ago.)

David was going to hike Mt. Adams, but I bribed him with the Twins, and he said, "Yes." The hike is eleven miles round trip up to South Twin at 4,700 feet and over to North Twin at 4,900 feet.

This made numbers thirty and thirty-one for me, and I'm hoping to get eight more in before snow flies. My goal is to finish next year and then have a huge yard sale of hiking and camping gear. David insists I'll keep hiking. He's hilarious that way.

I had picked up a new Columbia hiking shirt that is neon yellow. David said, "If we ever get lost, they will be able to find us from the Space Station." Jealous!

We took the North Twin trail. On the way up we crossed Little River three times. I don't like river crossings because I usually fall in. I have a sense of balance like a drunk on a rolling ship. David hops the rocks like a gazelle. Me? It's not pretty, folks. Old, unconditioned men don't exactly hop.

I stopped to hydrate, and another hiker passed me. David wasn't paying attention and he hiked the next tenth of a mile with that guy following him, all the while thinking it was me. Ha! Ha! Ha! Don't know what story he was prattling on about, but the other hiker put some serious distance between us after that.

Three times on the hike Satan tried to kill me. Each time I had to say, "David, get behind me." How he keeps taking the lead and then sprinting up a cliff is an enigma. Hospitals could do cheap stress tests by simply saying, "Follow that guy."

After picking up the North Twin Spur trail, we found the summit of North was socked in with clouds. All this time I thought it was Keith that attracted view-blocking clouds, but he wasn't there and the "aha" moment was sobering. I didn't mention it to David.

We waited 30 minutes for the clouds to break. It's the longest time David's ever spent on a peak. He's fidgety like that. We should have waited another fifteen minutes though because as soon as we headed down, we could see the clouds were gone and it had cleared up. Nonetheless, there were views from South that captured the entire Franconia Ridge. We could actually see seven 4,000 foot peaks.

On the way down, an area of the trail was littered with round rocks the size of baseballs. I hit one with my right foot and it sent me spinning, only for my left foot to land on another rock that had me falling backward into the bushes off the trail. While I was in mid-air, I swear I could hear David's camera clicking off frames. That is when you know you have an awesome hiking buddy.

We stopped at the river after eight miles because David had told me that soaking our legs in ice water would help them recover from the torture we had just subjected them to. After ten minutes in the water, my feet turned the color of a boiled lobster. The only thing that happened was now I couldn't feel my legs at all. That makes for real interesting hiking. I was walking on sticks that were not sending nerve messages to my brain. I guess it didn't matter because, at that point, my brain was responding with a busy signal.

When we arrived at the car, David produced a bottle of coconut lime water that his wife, Karen, had bought. He thought it was selfish of her to only buy one, so he took it. I was going to protest his treatment of his wife when he handed the bottle to me. It was rather tasty.

David is a great hiking buddy. The only thing that he ever complains about is that the mountains are not farther, steeper and higher. He needs to be hiking with 20-year-olds.

That brings up another hiking tip. Who to hike with? I would prefer to hike with people in their nineties. They're fun, full of stories, and in no rush. Make sure you have a lot in common. What if they like health food? No. What if they go to the gym all the time? No. What if they don't share their food? Hell, no! They also must be able to carry on a conversation by themselves, giving me the chance to keep breathing. Breathing is an art. It is necessary for life to continue. When my breathing starts getting labored, I know I'm doing too much. This usually starts right after I've lost sight of my car and continues until I see it again. I've learned a secret. Point at something off in the distance and when your companions are trying to figure it out, calmly turn away and attempt to regain normal breathing.

As Tom Hanks said in the movie *Cast Away*… "You gotta just keep breathing."

And that, my friend, is hiking.

27 THE STORY OF THE BONDS

As I have been journaling my experiences of hiking the New Hampshire forty-eight 4,000 footers, my advice to you now is: "For the love of God, don't do it." The Bonds are comprised of three mountains located in the middle of the Pemigewasset wilderness.

First is Bond Cliff at 4,265. The second is Mt. Bond at 4,698. The third is Bond West Peak at 4,540 feet. We were looking at a 24 mile in-and-out hike. Yikes! We changed our plan and decided to camp out so as not to hike it all in one day. An in-and-out hike meant we would have to do two of the peaks again on our way out, ending up summiting a total of five peaks.

My good hiking buddy, Keith Tilton, along with David Salois, Tim Mailloux, and Ian Kenney met at my house to make plans for what would be an overnighter camping trip. I was as excited as a five-year-old at Christmas. What a dope!

Although I was providing most of the necessary survival equipment, such as a stove and water purification system, no one wanted to help me carry it. That's okay because what doesn't kill you makes you stronger. Right? We decided that Keith, Ian and I would go on Friday afternoon, find a spot, and set up a camp. David and Tim would come in after work, hiking in with their headlamps.

We hiked in on the Lincoln Woods Trail. Remember as kids singing that song "This is the song that never ends. It just goes on and on my friends"? You just experienced the Lincoln Woods Trail!!! Five miles on an old railroad track that is a pain hiking in and the flipping Trail of Tears heading out.

The three of us found a nice spot about seven miles in and set up camp.

The other two goons arrived at 8 p.m. and kept us up till all hours of the night with all their noise and moving about. I couldn't tell if they were setting up hammocks or building a military facility. I finally got to sleep sometime in the wee hours of the morning only be awakened by Tim trying to build a fire at 3 a.m. Fires were not allowed! What was he thinking? Where are the bears when you need them? I just knew right then and there that this was going to be the granddaddy of all hikes.

Keith and Ian had already made up their minds that no matter how many bear warnings there were, they were going to keep their food in their tent. I cannot begin to tell you the anxiety this added to me as my tent was right next to theirs. But I shrugged it off and got a good three minutes of sleep anyway. I had brought a sleeping pill that I thought would give me an edge over all the other guys. However, after stopping at McDonald's on our way in and drinking two large glasses of Coke, the caffeine negated the effects of the sleep aid. The constant snoring of the other four guys not only kept the bears away but also ensured I did not get any rest before an incredibly grueling hike.

At 6 a.m. we woke up, broke camp and stuffed all our gear into our large backpacks and hid them in the woods. We took the essentials in our small packs and headed off at 7 a.m. for the Bataan Death March.

David was in a rush, so we skipped breakfast. YOU NEVER SKIP BREAKFAST!

My eyes were sunken in, my mouth was dry, my head hung down, my feet were dragging, and the hike had only started.

Of course, once again, I was leading point and getting a lot of groans and complaints at the fast pace that I was setting. After a long while and a vertical rock scramble, we summited Bond Cliff. The views were amazing, and I couldn't wait to get my picture taken on the famous Cliff's edge. Only two of five of the brave hikers were willing to go out there. After getting the picture, I made the mistake of looking down. Holy smokes! So that's what vertigo feels like. Ian said after he saw my widened eyes surrounded by a pale white face, he decided to forgo the cliff photo. I'm pretty sure I could feel some of my remaining brown hair turning grey. There is a slight depression on the rock where you stand on for the infamous photo, it always seems to have water in it. That ain't water, folks.

We descended back to 4,000 feet, only to head up a grueling 700 feet of incredibly steep boulders. We had made it to the top of Bond and were hydrating when the conversation turned to skipping West Bond and coming back to do it at another time. It was four against one, but by this time, I was determined to never come back into this corner of the world ever again. I insisted we make the last summit. The whining and crying were pathetic. I thought I was parenting all over again. We made the third summit and started heading back when David and Tim decided to go down to get water at the Guyot Campsite. It was a mere stone's throw away, but if you listen to them tell the story, you'd swear they had to hike into Maine and back.

After every summit, the trail would descend quite a ways, then we would have to climb back up to the next peak. Those ups and downs can really get to you.

By this time, we had been in the blistering sun and stifling humidity for hours and I was unaware I was beginning to suffer the effects of heat exhaustion. Heat exhaustion causes your mind to wander, gives you cramps and gas, and diminishes coherent conversation. That is why it is virtually undetectable (other than the gas). And yet I pushed on.

Although I had fallen into last place, I knew my only hope was to get below the tree line and into some shade. I ended up passing the crew and getting into the shelter of the trees. I could not stop sweating profusely, no matter how much I drank, and my breathing was deep and labored. My flesh was pale, and I had a temperature of 101° (not really, but it makes for a better story this way).

In the midst of this critical time, three members of the party wanted to quickly move on to get out of the woods, so they headed off and left me there to die like Leonardo DiCaprio in the movie *Revenant.* (The movie tells the story of Henry Glass, a mountain man who was left behind to die by his friends.)

I asked them to let Darlene know I loved her as I could feel life flowing out of me. Well, something was flowing out of me.

My old pal, Keith, refused to abandon me. I can't say enough about Keith. He has hiked almost all the 48 with me just to keep me from having to do them alone. He is always willing to let me set the pace and usually keeps his yawning to a minimum.

After sitting for a full 20 minutes and eating and hydrating, I somehow pulled enough strength together to ignore the dizziness and pushed on for the next four miles. Back at the campsite, I almost fainted twice and yet, I pushed on and purified enough water for Keith and me to do the last six miles with our full, heavy backpacks. Although Henry Glass survived by thinking of nothing but revenge, I pushed on wishing nothing but blessings on my teammates. It was their car I was hoping would explode in a huge ball of fire.

With nothing more than sheer determination, Keith and I started our final descent. We were passed by a couple of youngsters who were jogging this trail. I am certain that the state mental hospital has emptied its beds.

As we started out from our camp, I was contemplating the words of the ranger who had said that when you see a bear, put your arms out, speak softly, and start walking backward. A moment later I looked up the trail then turned to tell Keith there was a bear up ahead, but nothing would come out. All I could say was, "Ba, ba, ba…"

It turned out to be a rather large yellow lab who had rolled around in some black mud; its owners were only four seconds behind it. Those four seconds erased ten years off my life.

We still had five miles of flat hiking to endure as our backpacks were slowly pulling our shoulders clear off our bodies. Keith and I were in a state of override, no longer talking, just continually hiking. With two miles to go, I heard a loud pop and felt a stabbing pain in my left knee that made my leg buckle. I let out a small whimper that scared the deer in three states. Keith asked if I was okay without even turning around or slowing his pace. I don't blame him, as he was in a state of delirium and was walking on nothing but adrenaline and determination to survive. I, on the other hand, had severe pain that reduced my pace to a limp, and yet I still kept pushing myself to the extreme limits. I didn't know it at the time, but I had just torn my meniscus.

We had started hiking at 7 a.m. and it was now 7 p.m. We had gone 17 plus miles over five peaks.

Although the views and scenery were beautiful, I am glad I will never do it again as long as I live. EVER!

When I finally got home, Darlene said, "There, there," as she wiped my tears.

I snuggled in my Linus blanket and began icing my knee, hoping that I would be able to hike again in order to finish the last fourteen mountains.

David had tried to console me by reminding me how beautiful the views were. I responded that the views were losing their appeal as a reward. I now want hamburgers and ice cream at the top of each summit with a waterslide going down.

The guys I hike with are a great group of guys. Please do not hold ill will in your heart against any of them. Like Jesus, I can easily say, "Father, forgive them they don't know what they're doing." (Literally)

Beyond a doubt, this was the hardest hike I had ever done. I had never pushed myself to such extreme limits except for the time I asked a girl out on my first date.

It was a great time, and I'm glad I did it. The date that is. I never want to see another trail again.

Boy, that picture of me on Bond Cliff really came out great!

And that, my friend, is hiking!!!

28 THE STORY OF MT. CARRIGAIN

History records this mountain is named after Phillip Carrigain, NH Secretary of State (1805–10), but I can tell you right now it's named after a guy who forgot his wife's anniversary, birthday and name, so he headed into the wilds where she'd never find him. The Indians called this mountain 'Heapacrap' and they knew what they were talking about.

Three weeks ago, I finished hiking the Bonds, 24 miles covering five peaks. On that hike, I blew out my left knee, was in considerable pain, and had to limp out the last two miles. Had I been a horse, I know I would have gotten the bullet. Later that week, I went to a physical therapist who gave me stretching exercises to put my knee back together. I did them faithfully for two weeks, and my knee certainly recovered strength. In the third week, I began to moderately use my treadmill and elliptical machine when I wasn't eating ice cream. Thinking that I was conditioned, I set out to do Mt. Carrigain with my cheerful group of fellow hikers.

I have since found out it takes six weeks to be conditioned for any kind of sport or activity, however, you can lose all that conditioning within a mere two weeks. So after three weeks, I was totally unprepared to hike a 4,700 foot mountain that would end up being a ten and a half-mile hike. You know that old saying, "What doesn't kill you, makes you stronger"? That doesn't apply to these mountains. They may not kill you, but you'll wish they had.

This is a common mistake many hikers make. The old "I can do that one" syndrome. It comes from overestimating your physical condition while underestimating the brutality of these NH mountains. I was a classic sucker for the "I can do that one" syndrome.

We headed off to the great North at 5 a.m. Accompanying me on this hike was my good hiking buddy, Keith Tilton, along with David Salois, his daughter Holly, and Ian Kenney.

I had to endure jabs about my almost perfect driving all the way up to the mountains, but that's okay. It was just simply bantering going back and forth. By the way, the painted lines on the roads are just suggestions. I'm amazed at how quickly nice people like Keith and Ian can be influenced by bad behavior. Usually, these goons are all fast asleep, getting extra rest while I do all the driving. For some strange reason, on this trip north they were all wide awake their eyes resembling dinner plates. Ok, I may have been a little groggy and my driving may have been just a little off. Oh, for the record, I'm sorry for that one driver that ended up going off the road into the woods.

Upon arriving at the parking lot, we found out Holly's hydration bladder had leaked into her backpack, making it soaking wet. She was a real trooper and never even blamed her dad for not screwing the cap on tight enough. Though her pack did get her a little wet, she proved to be a powerful hiker. David, on the other hand, had miscalculated the temperature and was only wearing shorts with a jacket, hat, and gloves. You know you're in New England when you see people wearing down jackets with shorts.

Let me give you some advice on hydration bladders. After hydrating with water bottles for many hikes, I noticed that when I needed to stop, remove my pack, and get a bottle, my companions stood around staring at me like I was making them late for Walmart on Black Friday. I also noticed that they were not drinking. I thought, "Did I miss a camel hump implant surgery or something?" Always being in the front, I had missed seeing them sucking on a hydration tube like a 60's hippie sucking on a bong.

I'm the kind of guy that shares every new discovery to make life better with anyone who will listen. My "buddies"... not so. After my discovery, I headed to Eastern Mountain Sports faster than a guy that mistook Bengay for Preparation H. My new purchase??? A two-liter Camelback bladder. HA! Forget drinking and driving, now I can drink and hike and not lose any time. You do have to master the "not being able to breathe for ten seconds" while you drink. I learned that real fast after the first time I aspirated. It is kind of like waterboarding without the board.

So, we started the hike up the Signal Ridge Trail.

The first two miles were relatively flat, followed by three miles directly from Green Beret boot camp. I mean, we were going up at an unbelievable clip and the trail was strewn with rocks that made finding sure footing almost impossible. These were not the kind of rocks that you could hop from top to top. These jagged-edged rocks littered the entire three miles to the summit. It was like walking on shark's teeth. Hiking in this fashion made me tired. I needed to stop and recover more than I'd like to admit. In my defense, I had started the Keto diet. The dramatic changes in my body were sapping my energy. As I started falling behind, the insults began. I tried to encourage them to go on without me, as I would catch up. But poking fun at me was in season. I drew from experience and reserve strength that only God could supply, and I pushed on and summited with great form. I will admit, I was sucking air like a Craftsman shop vac fitted with an 8-cylinder Hemi. My heart was beating like a runaway jackhammer married to a machine gun, and I didn't know if I would make it off the mountain without a coronary episode.

People at the top were looking at my four companions as if to say, "Is he with you?" Of course, my companions acted as though they had never even met me.

Hiking with friends adds benefits that you miss when going solo. Friends can help you carry stuff if you are tired, lend a hand to get you over a technical rock formation or take that one in a million picture of you with a spectacular background.

I wonder what that would be like. The goons I hike with never do any of that. In fact, once, while I was slipping away from a gnarly rock formation, David's face appeared at the top and he smiled and said, "You got this," then disappeared. He's great for motivation that way. I did make it and it only took losing two fingernails and having a mild stroke.

The ridge trail at the summit was simply amazing. The fast-moving clouds laid down like a blanket at tree level you first hiked under and then into them. It was magical. A few minutes after we arrived on the summit, the clouds blew off and revealed the mountains and valley below in full Autumnal color. It was sheer beauty, one of the reasons people hike.

Even with overcast conditions we took some great pictures and headed back down with renewed energy. I set a pace that the other four could scarcely keep up with. I kind of feel bad about that. Oh, wait, no I don't.

The way down was horribly steep; after a while, I just wanted it to end. Again, the rock hopping totally drained the energy from my quads, and I was in incredible pain. And yet, I gritted my teeth and kept the pace to the end of the trail.

This is now summit 35 in my books, and I will never go back and do this mountain again, no matter what David says.

I wanted to get home quickly to rest, but somebody suggested we go across the Kancamagus Highway and enjoy the views with the other 40,000 leaf peepers. That decision added an hour and a half to our drive after we got stuck behind a nut in his motor home.

All in all, it was a great hike, even though the weather could have been better (and disregarding the constant insults). My hiking buddies are a good lot, and really do look out for each other. I know that they tease me in jest because, had it not been for me, they would have never found a way to cross that raging river. My exceptional hiking skills located the easiest route and got us all safely across. These mountains are getting farther, taller, and steeper, as I am nearing the end of the list. I hope with my knee condition I will be able to successfully complete this list.

I will immediately start reconditioning and getting ready for the next climb right after eating this bowl of ice cream.

Even though you swear you will never climb another peak, hiking does get into your blood like an infectious disease. The next thing you know, you're looking at your maps and comparing the mountains you have left on your list.

And that, my friend, is hiking.

I had asked others from the hiking community to share funny stories from their hikes. I only received this one from Kyle Tucker and share it now seeing that it took place on Mt. Carrigan.

I work two jobs and have little time to do any of these big mountains. When I finally get a chance it's hard not to go through with it. That being said, here is my story of Carrigain.

I've been long wanting to cowboy camp on top of a 4,000 footer. Just a sleeping bag under the stars on top of the mountains. So I finally picked a day to go. I wanted to do a sunset and sunrise hike with clear skies at night. That year we had a big heatwave in the nineties for about a week, and that's when I decided to go. I had checked the weather, and there was no chance of rain. It was going to be hot, and there was a small storm way up north that had a chance of hitting the top of New Hampshire, but that was it. So I packed my backpack with my sleeping bag, food, water, compass, flashlight, all the other stuff I'd need.

The trail guide said it was five miles with the first two and a half really flat. So I gave myself four hours to do the hike. As I drove up, I hit traffic, lots of traffic. There was an accident in the notch, and I lost valuable time. When I finally arrived, I now had about three hours to get to the top for sunset. I arrived at the road; it was closed. There is a parking lot off to the side where I parked. I met some people who said it was a two-mile walk along the road to get to the trailhead.

Ehh, ok, well, my bag is packed and I'm here, so screw it, I'm going. It happened to be one of the very few times I wore shorts. I started walking and instantly got eaten alive. I had forgotten the bug spray. I keep pushing and finally reach the trailhead; I have about an hour and a half left to the summit... not gonna happen, but my bag is packed and I'm here so, onward. I got through the flats pretty easily, and my map says there is a river crossing. But there is a fork in the trail and to go left before the river crossing. I get to the river, and I am surprised to find no fork. I've already started to get blisters, so I double up my socks.

I can't find the trail and debated on turning around, but my bag is packed, and I'm here, and I find what looks like a trail (it wasn't). Somehow, I bushwhacked and made it back onto the right trail. It's getting dark I've missed my sunset but, oh well, I keep going.

After it had gotten dark, a nice orange moon had risen that looked really cool, but also kind of eerie. As I got about three-fourths of the way up, I started seeing flashes, and I was not sure what's going on. Maybe I overexerted myself, and I was starting to see stuff. I just kept going.

Have you ever felt like a mountain didn't want you on it? Because this is how I was starting to feel. There were so many false peaks and I was still seeing flashes when I finally realized it was heat lightning. The lightning looked really cool through the trees with the moon above glowing orange. I finally broke tree line and could see all the mountains with the light of the moon and heat lightening. I made it to the tower. I'd done it! Yessss. I took all my gear off at the summit and laid down. But it's way too windy and I couldn't sleep there. I found another spot near the tower, off trail a little in a small hemlock grove, and threw the sleeping bag down and I was out. It was around 11:45 p.m. At 2:30 a.m.… BANG! I jumped out of my sleeping bag. What the hell was that? Just then there were three lightning strikes and crazy thunder. I had no tent because I wanted to cowboy camp. I was ok as long as it didn't rain. Drip, drip, drip. SHIT. The sky opened, so I grabbed all my stuff and ran back to the tower. I checked my phone (only place that has service on the whole mountain). The storm that was supposed to stay way up north was now an orange line of severe weather from Thornton all the way to Canada. I looked at the timetable to see when it would be over, and it was showing 7 a.m. Well, there went my sunrise. The question now became, do I wait it out or just head back? All my gear was now soaking wet and at least 20 pounds heavier, so I decided to make my way down and head out. About a mile and a half down I rolled my ankle on a rock and it was still pouring rain. I continued to work my way down and found I was now on a trail I didn't remember. It was the trail I was supposed to go up, but the fork was after the water crossing rather than before it. My headlamp was about to die because the batteries were only good for about three and a half hours, and I'd already changed them once. In my original plan, I wasn't supposed to be hiking in the dark at all. I got to the river crossing to find the water had risen a lot from all the rain. As I was crossing, I got to the last rock, lost my footing, and fell in. Now I was even wetter and still had four miles to go to get out. Ugh! My headlamp finally died but it was getting light out, so I could see just enough to keep going. I got to the trailhead, and it was still raining hard. I laid under the little map tower for about 20 minutes. My body was killing me. My toes were bleeding. I would have paid $1,000 to have anyone come and pick me up so I wouldn't have to do that road walk. lol

There was only one way out, so I started walking. Then the lovely bugs came back out. I was getting eaten alive again. The rain stopped, but now the heat and humidity were kicking in. I kept going. I got about halfway to the parking lot, and see a deer standing in the road. I was hunched over and swearing so much it would make a sailor blush when the deer looked at me and made an almost laughing noise. Then it slowly walked off. It was ironic and, cool all at the same time. I finally got to where I could see my car. I used all my energy to run to get to it and then couldn't find my keys. I had to dig through the backpack. All I wanted to do was sit down. I found them and the unlock button didn't work from being submerged in the river. So I had to go old school and use the key. The car door finally opened; I got in and took everything off:

shoes, socks shirt, pants. It was about 8:30 a.m. and I was sitting in my car in the parking lot, exhausted, wearing only my boxers. Do I sleep here for a little bit or just drive home? Well, the temp in my car was already 86°, so it looked like I was driving the longest drive of my life to get home. When I arrived, my girlfriend was surprised to see me back so early, and asked that since I was home early if I wanted to go to the fair? Absolutely not! lol

I slept in my chair with a bag of frozen peas on my ankle for the rest of the day.

Let me say it for Kyle... And that, my friend, is hiking.

29 THE STORY OF MT. ZEALAND

Zealand is named after the largest and most populous island in Denmark. How a NH mountain ended up with a Danish name is a mystery. Maybe the guy who charted this trail liked pastry for breakfast.

Or perhaps, some crazy Danish guy murdered his wife and wanted to stash the body somewhere no one would find it. As a matter of fact, when you make the summit, there is a small stack of stones that eerily looks like a grave marker.

After struggling with Mt. Carrigain a week ago, my legs felt like they had been run over by an 18-wheeler, then boiled in hot water. I was looking to redeem myself with a good, strong showing just seven days later. Mt. Zealand was the choice.

So I called my good hiking buddy, Keith Tilton, who, at first, made a crackling sound on the phone and said, "I can't hear you, you're breaking up." He's hilarious! Of course, he was up for the challenge after I found flaws in his four flimsy excuses. We had contacted some of the other goons, but they were all doing stupid stuff like working. Keith suggested we ask Dianna Smith, our church administrator, if she'd want to join in. She had started doing some of the 4,000 footers with her grandson and agreed to go with us.

I wasn't crazy about hiking with someone who was wearing psychedelic yoga pants, but it did give me a great idea for a Christmas gift for David Salois.

We left a little later than usual, around 6 a.m., Dianna drove. What a ride! I have twice as much gray hair now and my right hand won't stop shaking. Not to say she's a bad driver, but my hands were welded on the dashboard and my feet left two indentations on her floorboards. My facial expression was that of a 10-year-old watching the Exorcist for the first time. I don't know if I passed out from the G force on corners or from being so close to a rear license plate of the car in front of us that I could see fingerprints on it. I now have a twitch and a st-st-stutter.

We parked at the trailhead and headed up at about 8:15 a.m. My body was still trembling as we started the hike.

Early on, we could see the summit was socked in by low clouds which is par for the course when you're hiking with Keith Tilton. Views become irrelevant. He is a magnet for bad weather.

Here's a little hiking tip I learned from my son, Tim. As soon as you can, take your Nalgene bottle out while it's still cold and offer everyone some of your water. The results are that half-way up your water is depleted and you are no longer carrying all that weight. Then you get to sip from everyone else's water as needed as they bear the weight throughout the remainder of their hike. Ha! Ha! The apple doesn't fall far from the tree.

The first two and a half miles were relatively flat. There were sections of boardwalks and scenic fall foliage views. After a while, we made it to the Zealand Hut. What a great place! I have yet to spend a night at a hut, but it's definitely on the to-do list. From the hut we got some great pictures of the Notch and then headed up. Now, when I say headed up, I mean that the next two miles were like taking off in an F-35 fighter jet. It went up at break-neck pitch. We encountered some ladder systems and places where technical rock formations required the skilled point person (myself) to lead the way so the others could follow safely. This trail had it all.

Having only stopped twice during the ascent, I realized I was once again in condition to hike these bad boys of the White Mountains. I know there are young, athletic, hikers reading my stories who cannot relate to my trials. Let me just say, I hate you.

The trail leveled off again for about another mile and a half and slowly made its way to the main summit. The trail was now a lot of fun even in the fog and wind. It seemed like what wasn't slab rock was mud. There were no views at the overlook because of the clouds and there were no views at the summit because it never broke the tree line. Even with that, the hike was cordial, and the conversation polite and courteous. I was wondering why this hike was so different, when it dawned on me. David Salois was not with us to instigate the bantering that usually takes place. Every person brings a certain spice to hiking. Each in their own way adds to the memories of a good hike. I'm told people enjoy hiking with me because of the serious, athletic, no-nonsense approach I have towards hiking.

I will say that the most discouraging part of the hike was being passed by two women, one in her 70's and the other one in her 80's. These people have no business being on these kinds of trails and should be confined to hiking on the beach. Don't these ladies know I still have a small amount of male ego to protect? However, the highlight was on the way down when I passed seven people on the trail. That's right me, seven, passed!!!

Keith will try to tell you that they were all lame or injured in some way, but don't believe him for a minute. They were healthy senior citizens in every respect.

Overall the trip was an excellent hike, and we encountered some very scenic beaver ponds, waterfalls, and rock formations.

I had packed well and had the gear necessary to face the wet fog and the 20 miles an hour wind. Keith did just fine in his T-shirt.

Dianna turned in a good showing and matched the pace I'd set. She and Keith hardly yawned at all but playing Yahtzee while hiking gets a little tedious.

This turned out to be a fun hike and someday I'll do it again… NOT!

And that, my friend, is hiking.

30 THE STORY OF
MT. HANCOCK & SOUTH HANCOCK

The Hancocks are named after John Hancock who was one of the founding fathers of our country. You've heard people say, "Put your John Hancock here," meaning, of course, your signature. Well, when you start climbing these mountains, you might as well sign your life away.

I knew there would be issues when I asked David Salois if he wanted to hike on Friday. When he heard we were doing the Hancocks, he started coughing and sniffling and made up a story of a sudden cold that had miraculously settled in just one minute ago. When he does that, you know that you are in for a doozy of a hike.

Ian Kenney said that he would solo hike it that Saturday. All I can say is, "Good luck with that, Ian." SAR will do the recovery.

Of course, my good hiking buddy, Keith Tilton, was ready to be picked up at 6 a.m. and make the drive to the great North. A quick stop at Dunkin's and some banter about what we thought we'd encounter on the hike up. I don't know about others, but as I start getting into the Whites, I begin to see how big these mountains are. It always starts getting me nervous. Kind of like the soldiers of WWI going over the top never knowing if they'd make it back.

I'm usually not a nervous type, but if my imagination starts running away from me, it'll do a four-minute mile every time. I had heard they were steep, but even my wild imagination could not have dreamed up what lay ahead.

After arriving, we noticed the area had gotten about half an inch of snow. The drop in temperature made for a very icy climb. Water that usually runs down these trails had frozen.

This is where the right equipment is a necessity. I have Hillsound trail crampons with 5/8th-inch spikes. They are awesome! The box says they are for hiking, trail running, and glacier traveling. I usually stick to hiking, because the other two are not options for a 60-year-old who wants to see 61. I also own two pairs of snowshoes because postholing is the anathema of winter hiking. Want to start great conversations? Next time you're in a room full of hikers, tell them how you post-holed all the way down a mountain. It'll be great fun.

We hiked in almost three full miles on fairly level ground and a nice trail. The scenery of the NH woods covered in freshly fallen snow is amazing. It's better for mental health than anything else. I think some of the world's problems are that too many people never get out into the great outdoors.

Other than hearing Keith complain about how cold it was, this was a good hike.

After gaining altitude for some time, I saw North Hancock in the distance and realized I had to descend all the way down into the valley only to trudge back uphill to regain the lost altitude.

Don't ever believe the altitude markings on maps when they make it look relatively flat. There is no such thing. We reluctantly went into the valley. Keith has a little saying, "You have to go down to go up". I've heard it a thousand times. If he ever goes missing, you'll know I heard the phrase one too many times. Then we started going up. I mean one of the steepest ups that we've done so far, for about 1,400 feet. Imagine a ladder made of boulders and covered with roots turning into sections of slab rock with no footing going up 1,400 feet, and you've pretty much got the idea. Part of this trail had so many roots that Alex Haley could write another novel.

Here's another tip you can take to the bank. How to stay on a trail. It is very important to have good maps. Darlene bought me the AMC White Mountain NF Trail map set. They cover every mountain and all the trails. They are waterproof and tear-resistant, and I use them constantly. There are also apps for your phone, such as AllTrails which Ian uses; it has kept us on trails in freshly fallen snow. Most trails have painted blazes on rocks or trees, but others lack these helpful markers. Most of the time the trail is so well traveled that it is hard to miss. Sometimes river crossings can be confusing because the trail goes up both sides of a river as people are looking for a safe way to cross. Make sure you pick up the correct trail on the other side.

If you happen to get lost. Just start running as fast as you can all the while dropping your gear and clothing and you will be just fine.

On some of the steeper, rocky Terrifying 25 trails, the markings may be nonexistent, but you can usually follow the poop and bloodstains left behind by the previous hikers.

I stopped to rest about three times on the way up. Each time was to bring my breathing back to something that would resemble a normal human being. We saw a Gray Jay, in bird language, I could discern that he was saying, "Turn around now. Turn around now."

But Keith and I just kept going. There were no levels, no switchbacks, nothing but up. After what seemed like an eternity of climbing, we reached the ridge trail and headed to the summit. We were pretty disappointed with the lack of decent views. Now you need to understand what hiking with Keith is like. If you hike a mountain that has 360-degree views, you're guaranteed to be socked in with clouds. But, if you hike a mountain that has no or few views, it is going to be one of the nicest days of the year. I tell you; he's cursed.

We then crossed over the mile-and-a-half ridge trail to the other summit. It was a gorgeous hike with a real wintertime feel. I started singing Christmas carols until I saw Keith pick up a large stick. I could clearly see by the look in his eye that the strain of climbing had taken its toll on the old guy. There were about two inches of snow on the ground, but again, very limited views at South Hancock.

As we hiked from one summit to the other, we noticed all the tracks in the snow going in the opposite direction. Everyone we met was going in the opposite direction. They told us they had read to go up to South and come down North Hancock. After our experience and much discussion, Keith and I agreed that we went the easier way. Both were really steep, but the descent we went down was two-tenths of a mile shorter. When I say, "went down", I mean that even mountain goats and deer die on this mountain. I saw a raccoon that was so scared by the time he went 30 feet down, he turned black and white and looked like a skunk. The footing was horrible, snowy and icy, and very, very steep. With every step I took, I imagined Darlene placing another flower on my casket. By the time I reached the bottom, the picture in my mind was of an acre field, six feet deep with flowers, and my casket somewhere in the middle. I don't tell Darlene half of these stories or let her see half of the pictures for fear she will stop me from enjoying these little adventures. I re-injured my knee going down because each step had to be calculated for supporting my weight without slipping. This caused more stress on the joint than normal.

We met a guy on our way down who was going up. We couldn't believe it when he passed us again, now heading out. We asked him, "Did you do the whole Loop?" He said, "Yes." He told us that he had just finished the Appalachian Trail two weeks ago and his legs were in really good condition. His legs looked like tree trunks. He was like a 2019 Corvette, while I was similar to a 1976 Ford Pinto that had just run out of gas.

Every time I am passed by hikers in their 20's or 30's, it makes me wonder why I didn't do this earlier. But then again, being elderly, overweight and out of shape adds to the challenge and increases the value of that dang patch.

When we got back to the car, I noticed my down jacket smelled like a goose had crawled in it and died. It was really nasty. I can't understand why, I just washed it last winter. I sprayed it with Odoban and now think it's good for another year.

Darlene doesn't understand the delicate care of gear as I do. In fact, she wants to wash my clothes after every hike.

I only have ten more mountains to do to finish this bucket list and I can't wait. (Even though I did notice another list called 'The 52 with a View'.)

And that, my friend, is hiking.

31 THE STORY OF MT. CARTER DOME

After straining my knee coming down the incredibly steep Hancocks, I was taken out of hiking for quite some time for recuperation. There was a strange sensation in my knee that most people refer to as acute, unbearable pain.

After several weeks off, Keith and I hiked Mount Kearsarge, which is a 3,000 footer. My knee performed fairly well. Then I thought, "Hey, why not do a ten-mile round trip in the deep snow up the 4,700 foot Carter Dome?" This is a condition known to doctors as being psychotic delusional. This is when the hiking disease is reaching its zenith. By this time your eyes have changed color. Your hair sticks out in clumps. You drool a lot and constantly think about hiking.

I started calling some of the goons I hike with and found out all of them were on board. That is until David Salois came up with this lame excuse about a carpenter who had to do some work on a garage he doesn't even have, and Ian Kenney started having some second thoughts about a winter hike. So that left my good old hiking buddy, Keith Tilton, and Brett Hazelwood with his bear of a dog named Eli.

I woke up at four in the morning. I wouldn't do that even if my house were on fire but to hike? You betcha.

Brett decided to drive his own vehicle. I think the other guys may have shared some exaggerated stories about my driving. I went to pick up Keith and we headed off to the great North Woods... in the dark.

The day before, the windchill on Carter Dome was 40 below zero. But today was a beautiful day, sunny, hardly any wind, and a balmy 37 degrees at the base and 20° at the summit. Perfect winter conditions!

We hit the trail and it was a snow-covered winter wonderland. Two miles in we encountered a river crossing. Now remember in hiking, they usually put the most skilled, strongest, most experienced, and I might say best looking, in the front to discover all the tricky areas. Of course, I'm always up for the challenge. However, on this tricky river crossing the water was a little high and the rocks quite icy and covered in snow. I made it all the way across to the other side when I slipped off the bank and plunged my left leg knee-deep into brisk winter water. The water quickly came into my boot like it was the Titanic. My two layers of socks were soaking wet and my first thought was, "My hike is over." So I crossed the river again to discuss the situation with my companions. They were reluctant to go on without me leading the way, but I pressed them hard to continue on their own. Just then another hiker came and asked if I had dry socks, which, of course, I did because I carry everything when winter hiking. He then asked if I had plastic bags to put over my socks to keep the water in the wet boot from soaking the dry socks. OK, so I don't carry everything. I didn't have plastic bags, but he gave me some that were just a little small. I was really thankful. Most hikers are awesome people who go out of their way to help people like me. We decided to press on. By the time I'd hiked another mile, I decided it was time to change my socks, unfortunately, the tiny bags kept ripping.

I may add that 91% of people turn around at this point. But we were having fun and the temps were mild. So onwards we went!

As we trudged forward, the hike started to feel like it would go on forever. My breathing became labored like a dying man with an apple stuck in his throat, and my heart was fluttering like a drunken butterfly. I was slipping on the loose snow which sapped my strength faster than a rabbit on crack. I was also sweating a lot, a potential problem if the weather changed on us. It was then, about a mile from the summit, that we started postholing. Postholing is when you're walking on a packed-down snowshoe trail, but then your feet start sinking through the monorail and you fall in up to your knee. It takes an incredible amount of strength and energy to keep digging yourself out, especially when it starts happening every ten steps. We stopped after three postholes and I put on my dry socks, threw a couple of hand warmers into my boot and put on my snowshoes. I'd like to say that everything changed, but I was still gasping for air and trying to keep my heart inside my chest cavity. There is quite a controversy between postholers and snowshoers within the hiking community, mostly from snowshoers who don't like to see their nicely packed trails turned into Swiss cheese. The banter back and forth can be amusing. I've decided to be diplomatic and wear snowshoes while admiring the strength of the other *&%#&@ guy who postholed all the way up Carter Dome.

The snowshoes prevented postholing, but they also caused you to walk just a little differently, thus fatiguing muscles you did not know you possessed.

163

We finally summited just as my rubberized legs were starting to fail. We took some great photos of beautiful winter scenery and the Presidential Range. I also shot some spectacular video; while watching it later that evening I discovered the audio sounded like an obscene phone call. I understand the best solution is to wait until your breathing returns to normal before filming. Unfortunately for me, that doesn't happen until halfway home on Route 93.

The mountains in winter conditions are pristine and have an entirely unique beauty. There tend to be fewer hikers and NO BUGS! Brett was getting cold and wanted to get out quickly, so he took off. Most people stay warm by moving but when they hike with me the pace is quite slow. I could deal with Keith and Brett playing card games as they crawled behind me, but their laying down to make snow angels was starting to get irritating.

Keith and I finally started down after some trail food and water. Staying hydrated in the winter is important because you lose a lot of moisture to the dry winter air, not to mention sweating like a freak because of trudging through the snow.

My pace was the speed of molasses running uphill on a cold day. After a while I decided to remove my snowshoes, only to discover that the trail was getting mushy and very slippery. I wiped out at least three times. The last time was right in front of a woman hiker who had stepped off the path to let us go by. I tried to make it look like the fall was intentional so as not to bruise my male ego, but I think the air leaving my lungs as the wind was knocked out of me may have given the whole thing away. That was pretty humiliating, so I stopped and put on my spikes, which are like bear teeth, for better traction. No problem with slipping after that.

Every now and then you get to witness a phenomenon in the wild that stays with you forever. On this hike, it was the memorable wipeout of Keith. Let me break it down for you. As we were coming down the Nineteen Mile Brook trail, there were two blowdowns across the trail. One was about four feet off the ground, and the other a foot off the ground but only three feet after the first one.

Because I'm not a flexible kind of guy, I got on all fours and crawled under the first blowdown. Then I used the second one to help me stand back up. Gumby, or should I say Keith, started right in by laughing and using derogatory remarks about my comical hiking style as he folded right in two like a yoga master only to stand up and trip over the second tree. He performed the most awesome face plant I have ever witnessed. Although it was only a nanosecond after his face sank into the snow, I had drawn my phone faster than Clint Eastwood skinning his six-shooter in *Outlaw Josey Wales*. Keith shot out of the snow like he had hit a trampoline, both arms spinning like propellers in an attempt to brush off all the evidence before I got the picture. I had actually gotten three. For the rest of the hike, he accused me of not helping, but only taking pictures of the misadventure, laughing and then sprinting away. I vehemently denied his view as my legs no longer had the ability to sprint.

Keith soon got over his bad feelings as I pointed out how the only time he took his camera out was when I was crossing that dang river on the return journey? He just wanted to capture me falling in the water... again.

It seemed like the trail would never end and my knee was stiffening up like a rusted hinge. We continued on in silence because neither one of us really had the strength to talk anymore. I started cursing winter hiking and swearing I was never going to do this again because the rest of the hikes I had to do were even longer.

There is something about imitating *The Walking Dead* as you limp into the parking lot, seeing your car and starting to cry. Real men are not afraid of tears, but the whimpering sounds did attract some attention. It was then, as I was contemplating taking up the winter sport of figure skating, that my mind drifted to the possibility of doing the other two Carter Mountains in this range sometime this winter.

And that, my friend, is hiking!

.

32 THE STORY OF MIDDLE CARTER

I am done with hiking! Everyone has limits and I have exceeded mine. Let me tell you how it all came about.

A few weeks ago, Keith, David, Ian and I attempted to do Middle and South Carter via the Imp Trail. Middle Carter is 4,600 feet. It is named after a man who hunted on these mountains and who still hunts humans to this day by wearing them down and watching them slowly die on his hills.

On our first attempt, we started at a balmy three below zero. My fingers were already frozen before leaving the parking lot because my snowshoe bindings were frozen stiff from being in the trunk of my car. By the time we hit 3,200 feet, it was at least 15 below zero with a forecast of 25 to 40 below zero. That is colder than a well digger's nipples. That is when people die. By now my jaw was frozen and I couldn't say anything intelligible. Of course, my hiking companion would say that that's a normal condition.

I could see the possibility of impending doom and suggested we turn back. Well, that went over like a fart in church. There was some cordial debate; eventually, we all agreed to call it a day. This turned out to be a life-saving decision. I can't tell you how many times I saved everyone's life in this fashion.

I had a spectacular wipe-out on the way down, reminiscent of the commercial line, "I've fallen and can't get up!" With my right snowshoe, I had stepped on an 18" diameter blowdown running parallel to the trail and hidden beneath the snow. My foot slid off causing me to fall to the right of the blowdown and leaving my left leg and snowshoe hooked on the other side. I found myself laying

on a rather steep slope falling away from the trail in snow so deep there was nothing solid beneath me to use to push myself back up. The more I wiggled, the deeper I sank.

After uncontrollable belly laughing and the wiping away of tears, my friends took pictures and filmed video before eventually helping me out. My buddies are the best.

By the time we got to the parking lot, there were lots of frozen fingers and toes.

As we planned for a second assault, the forecast was calling for winds at 50 to 60 miles an hour with gusts up to 70. Seeing how I wasn't interested in parasailing off a mountain, we didn't even go.

I thought I would get ready for the next attempt by wearing four-pound ankle weights for four days straight and even working out in them. I was ready. My legs? Not so much.

The second attempt happened on a day with a forecast of sunny skies at 20 to 30 above zero and hardly any wind.

I called my old hiking buddy, Keith Tilton, and Ian Kenney and David Salois, who, unfortunately, had to work ... again. Lucky for him.

We headed off at 5 a.m. to the Great North Woods.

We started the hike at 7 a.m. wearing spikes. However, there was just enough freshly fallen snow to make them almost ineffective. The higher we got, the deeper the snow became, so eventually we switched over to our snowshoes. Walking five miles in snowshoes is not exactly fun. Especially when you're always the point person, breaking the trail for the other guys.

We did the first 3.2 miles in about an hour and a half. The next mile took us almost two hours. It was the mile from hell. It went through spruce trees that were bent over with layers of frozen snow over smaller spruce trees buried in snow that would suck you down into the center of the earth. It was a combination of hiking and fighting off demon trees that would not bend. When you're postholing while wearing snowshoes you know you're in the battle of a lifetime.

We eventually made it to the ridge trail looking like we'd done five rounds with a professional kickboxer. We went on to summit Middle Carter. South Carter was a little over a mile away which would have added two more miles to our hike. We were pretty tired, so we called it. I hated turning around, but safety first in the mountains.

As we descended, I really needed my poles to hold my fat body back and save my knees and legs from the stress. However, the snow was four feet deep at the summit, and my poles vanished into the abyss and became useless. My summer poles did not have snow baskets. The sinking pole trick left my quads and knees to do the work and, after a couple of miles, they were shot. I was becoming tired and no longer in my usual cheerful mood. The pain in my legs was somewhere between pure burning fire and whatever else you can imagine worse than that.

You also need to know something about these beautiful, little evergreen trees on the tops of mountains. They have survived by being the gnarliest, toughest little plants on the planet. They do not budge. When you try to push them out of the way, they push you back right off the trail so that you post-hole and sink out of sight. They will slash your face and your hands, hook your clothing, and snag and trip your snowshoes. If you try to snap a branch to move it out of your way, good luck. They don't break. I think they make airplane black boxes out of these trees.

The more tired I got, the more my mood turned sour. Right as I was trying to jump a small creek, I post-holed and went right down into it. I screamed out loud, "Son of a biscuit." The sound literally echoed off the mountains.

Keith and Ian will say that they heard something else, but that's because their minds are always on bad words that I would never use.

By this time my bad knee had swelled up like a Zeppelin and was clicking like Yahtzee dice in the shaker can. I was so tired! Every muscle I had, and some I didn't know existed, were painfully sore.

Then it happened. I snapped one of my Black Diamond trekking poles.

It must have gotten caught on a rock under the snow and, as I had walked past it, I pulled it sideways rather than up and "snap". There goes another $120.

Keith was kind enough to let me use one of his. I am going to have to get better winter poles that have snow baskets on them. I'm pretty sure by the time I'm done buying all the equipment and clothing necessary, I could have bought my own mountain.

The trail back to the parking lot seemed endless. I urged my companions to go on without me and let me die in peace. But they never listen. This hike brought back memories of my first hike up Mt. Waumbec and quickly became one of the top three worst hikes of all times.

The physical demands of winter hiking had conquered my emotional defenses.

By the time we reached the car, my thought life was nothing to be proud of. I was done with winter hiking. I was done with hiking. I was just plain done!

My legs felt like they had been on the stretching racks. My left knee was telling me it wasn't right. I think my most demoralizing thought was that I would have to go all the way back up to do South Carter.

Right when you're figuring out how much you can sell your gear for, you get that little thought that creeps in like a fox and says, "I wonder what the weather will be like next week?"

And that, my friend, is hiking.

On a positive note that was number 40 and leaves me with only eight more torture sessions and then I'm done. And I mean DONE!!!

33 THE STORY OF MT. GALEHEAD

Mt. Galehead is named after Suzanna Gale an early pioneer with an unusually large head. In fact, the Indians called her 'So-shamobuck' which means "head like wrecking ball". To escape bullying she built a cabin on top of this mountain. One day she fell into the river and because her head was so big, she drowned. The river was then named the Galehead River. The mountain was named Mt. Galehead, and the cabin is called the AMC Galehead Hut. To this day, there is an 85 pound pillow in the hut. I'm not making this up. You can Google it.

Anyway, it had been seven months since my last attempt at a 4,000 footer. I had injured my knee on the Bonds, then again on the Hancocks, then again on Middle Carter, then again by postholing in the Belknap Range.

After an MRI and X-rays, it was determined to be a torn meniscus, arthritis and, like Suzanna, a big head. I was counseled to buy a knee brace that took the pain away by costing so much my mind was occupied with wondering how I would afford to eat for the next six months.

The new bionic brace did work, and I spent the winter completing the Belknap Redline. That's another patch I've earned. I don't mention it much because my hiking partners are extremely jealous.

The time had come to tackle my forty-first 4,000 footer. For now, my knee condition makes it a one mountain at a time ordeal. I really hope I can finish all forty-eight without knee replacement or a lobotomy.

I had been warned on numerous occasions that Mt. Galehead is a steep one. That thought settled into my imagination and tormented me for days.

My old hiking buddy, Keith Tilton, said that he would go with me, even though he'd already hiked Mt. Galehead. That's a true friend. My other two buddies, Ian and David came up with lame excuses like having to work. Those guys are so funny. I don't know why their employers fail to recognize the importance of hiking.

This hike had perfect NH conditions: freezing cold weather with wind and a chance of rain. As they say in the northern parts, if you don't like the weather, wait a minute.

The trail started off easy, then changed to mud, to mud with roots, to rock, and finally to a staircase of boulders. I'm not making this up.

The whining and complaining were horrible, but Keith threatened to leave so I retreated to murmuring.

We summited after a non-stop hike. The winter conditioning seemed to have paid off.

The Galehead Hut is an amazing place to kick back and enjoy the views of the notch. Although it's a great place for a photo op,

I'm not that photogenic and most of my pictures come out looking like I have an incurable disease.

Just as we arrived at the hut so did two young forestry workers. I think they ran up the trail with full packs and construction tools. They dropped their packs and took their tools, smiled and said "Hi," then disappeared up the trail just to clean it up for Keith and me. They probably saw that he was struggling and wanted to get rid of any blowdowns that would impede his hike. These two young people had legs like oak trees. Mine are like saplings and it really gave me a complex. Once someone saw me hiking in shorts and asked if I had a license to ride that chicken.

I've really got to hand it to these workers as they are all over these mountains cleaning them up and making repairs so the rest of us can enjoy ourselves.

Always remember to keep the mountains clean. Pack out what you pack in. If you throw out trash you might end up going missing. Permanently!

On the way down, we stopped again at the hut for some snacks and got held up and robbed by a Gray Jay. That's the first time I'd ever seen Keith share anything with anyone.

Here is another hiking tip. What you pack for food is extremely important. Pizza is good as well as hotdogs and French fries. Seriously though, there are tricks to the trade that have worked for me. I like putting the Propel drink mix in my water. It adds salts and electrolytes and other scientific junk that you need and gives you a boost along with incredible gas. Keith insists the gas is natural for me and not from the Propel. I also carry chewable Shot Blocks and paste Shot Blocks that do the same thing (except for the gas). I find that I sweat enough to fill a child's swimming pool and, though water is necessary, it doesn't replace those things I am losing. Everything I read says always bring more than you need, so I'm at the place now that I carry enough snacks to survive for a month. Sometimes I will bring a twelve-ounce Boost chocolate shake. Again, it helps, and I need all the help I can get. Stingers and trail mix are always good, as well as plastic bags filled with spaghetti and meatballs. Don't forget the straw.

As we began our nonstop descent, we heard a helicopter and saw that it was carrying a cargo net of supplies to the hut. Five times it made its supply run. I found out later they radioed from the hut and asked the chopper to wait until Keith had left because he looked like he'd eat it all before they could even get it stored away.

Anyway, we finished the ten miles and 4,052 feet hike in record time. One of my best ever!

I was exhausted and nodded off twice on the drive home... as I was the driver, I didn't bother informing Keith because he already has a nervous condition from my driving.

I got home, drank gallons of water, ate everything in sight, then slept like a baby.

We're planning another hike, hopefully with Ian and David, but there's no need to share my driving narcolepsy events. These guys are already wound pretty tight.

As long as the knees hold out, I'll keep plugging away at the last seven peaks to finish the forty-eight.

By the way, the weather turned out to be spectacular right down to the breeze that kept the black flies away.

It was an epic day.

And that, my friend, is hiking.

34 THE STORY OF SOUTH CARTER

So my old hiking buddy, Keith Tilton, and I decided to head north for some R&R. For those of you who are not hikers, you may think R&R means rest and recuperation, but for those of you who hike in the Whites, you know that really stands for rocks and roots.

I picked Keith up at 6 a.m., and he surprised me with an egg sandwich. I didn't have the heart to tell him I had just finished four waffles, so I ate the sandwich, figuring I could use the extra fuel as we were getting ready to hike a 4,430 foot mountain on a nine and a half-mile stroll in 84° heat. The choices of what to hike were getting thinner, and I kept putting off the ones I really dreaded. South Carter was the last remaining hike that I considered survivable. I was hoping to enjoy this one because the remaining mountains scared the bejeebies out of me.

We arrived at the parking lot and headed up the Nineteen Mile Brook Trail. The weather was perfect. The trail started off at a gradual incline for about two miles, getting steep before we picked up the Carter Dome Ridge Trail. That is when the fun began. We experienced standing water, mud, blowdowns, and steep sections that were incredibly rocky - typical New Hampshire mountain hiking!

I hike with a pair of Black Diamond hiking poles. I think their name comes from the fact that you could buy actual diamonds or the poles. You've heard the saying "Weebles wobble but they don't fall down?" Well, I may be full of bull, but I fall quite a bit. I don't know why but I have a terrible sense of balance. I've tripped over rocks, roots, stumps, and even my own hiking poles. I've used the poles to help keep my balance as I'm falling. I've seen them bend like a British longbow, and spring me right back up again. Keith says I trip because I'm clumsy and uncoordinated. There may be some truth to that, so I decided to take a dance lesson once to help me develop finesse and balance. At the end of the hour lesson the dance instructor's ankle had to be taped up; she refunded my money and asked that I leave and never come back. Geez, cut me some slack.

I also use my poles in case of a bear attack. I have seen lion trainers use a stool because the legs confuse the lion, and it doesn't know what the threat is or where it's coming from. I figure if a bear attacks, I will hold my poles pointed in its direction causing the bear to lose its frame of reference. Maybe it will forget there's a great big piece of human flesh that's tinkling in his pants at the other end of the poles. I have yet to try this tactic, as I have not seen a bear. But in theory I believe it will work.

We encountered a lot of blowdowns. Blowdowns are when Mother Nature sneezes and knocks over a tree. It seems Mother Nature had a full out nasal hissy fit on the top of South Carter

I am six feet three inches tall. Did I mention it was hot? Whoever you angels are who cut away the blowdowns, please cut the ones that go across the trail at six feet high. I smacked my head on a blowdown going across the trail. I was wearing a hat with a visor and looking down at my footing when... wham. My eyes crossed, my knees buckled, and I saw stars for a moment. The thud reverberated throughout the entire Carter Range. It was so loud that within five minutes, a coyote came rushing to the area ready to do the dance with what he thought was a free meal. Up went the hiking poles pointing in his direction to put him off guard. He wandered away, a little confused. I wandered off, staggering from the knot on my head.

We met some other hikers on the trail, most of whom were between 20 and 30, full of energy and smiles. What a bunch of weirdos! I can't stand them. If you're not gasping and heaving and sucking in every molecule of oxygen your lungs can take, then you're not doing it right and shouldn't be on these mountains.

We made our last push to the top over steep and rocky terrain. Did I mention it was hot?

When we finally found the summit, we saw that there was one cairn that marked the summit, but it had been knocked over by a blowdown. The irony of ironies!

As we started our descent, we were joined by our old friends the black flies. What would a hike be without these little blood-sucking vampires swarming you by the millions? Did I mention it was hot?

As we were going through a section of blowdowns, there was a branch sticking out that jabbed me in my right shoulder. I yelled out "son of a biscuit". I felt that was good composure because inside my head it was more like #@^$#*&>$# stupid branch. I have a photo of the brutal flesh wounds I received as evidence.

In the past, my new bionic knee brace had been chafing the tendons behind my knee. On this hike, it had rubbed the flesh raw. If anyone ever points at it and says, "Ewwwwww," I'll just say, "It's leprosy. Now get away."

I have heard you can tell you are getting dehydrated by the color of your pee. What does it mean when it looks like orange Kool-Aid? Note to self, when it's going to be 84°, bring more hydration!

We were descending alongside a river when Keith suddenly decided to cross. I didn't understand why. Then he stood there looking at me like I was on the wrong side of the river. Now I don't know if he did that accidentally, or if he was trying to get away from my complaining about the heat. Anyway, I convinced him he was on the wrong side of the river, and he had to return by doing some pretty technical rock hopping. It's amazing how fast you can hop rocks when the guy driving the car starts heading down the trail.

On our way down we were passed by three women roughly our age. Now granted, they'd only hiked a couple of miles up the trail and didn't do a 4,400 foot mountain, but still to be passed by these women was wounding to my personhood. I deduced that the only logical explanation was that they were all on crack. Such a shame that it affects even the elderly. SMH.

After I got home, I spent some time icing my knee while reminiscing about the swell hike I had with my buddy, Keith. I'm hoping he secretly didn't get those ladies' phone numbers as he may be looking for new hiking partners.

I have noticed he's developed a funny eye twitch.

And that, my friend, is hiking.

35 THE STORY OF THE WILDCATS

Two more are in the books. Today was a great hike. Why? Because I'm alive and home writing about it after being convinced I'd never live to see another sunrise. But I'm getting ahead of myself.

The Wildcats begin at Wildcat D then go to C, B and finally A. Wildcat D stands at 4,062 feet and Wildcat A at 4,032 feet. This was a nine-mile hike in 77° heat that began with two and a half miles straight up a ski slope. There is a steep trail that most people who aren't scaredy-cats take, but I decided against it from a fear of falling and breaking something.

When I sent out the text invitations to my hiking buddies. David Salois immediately responded with one word... S T E E P.

Keith and Ian jumped on the invite because there was a one day break in the monsoons we used to call June.

David said that he had to work. I've learned that when David gives a warning followed by reasons why he can't go, it usually means we could die on that trail. I called his boss and he said it was so slow he was thinking of giving everyone the day off. Ha, that David. He's a riot.

I knew it would be a tough day because my new coffee spot was not open. No coffee, no breakfast sandwiches. What's this world coming to? I was a tad early picking up Keith and Ian, so I shot up to Dunkins. As I came back, I accidentally drove past Keith's house. He's got one of those driveways that, unless you've lived there for 20 years, is easy to miss. Of course, he and Ian were both in the yard watching me drive past, pointing and laughing. Oh, what fun banter we had on the trip north. Then we drove right past Wildcat Ski Resort. How can you miss that? It was going to be one of those days.

We hit the slopes (pun) and in the direct sunlight, it was a killer. We had decided to do the Pole Cat Trail. I soon felt sluggish and had to stop. A lot. A real lot.

My inability to breathe made me wonder if I'd ever get used to this hiking thing.

Finally, we summited Wildcat D.

We took great pics, and the wind was refreshing.

Then we hit the trail. S T E E P!

One section was so steep that Ian and I admitted that had either of us been alone, we would have jumped ship. Hiking with others pushes you to do things you wouldn't do alone; like get up at 4 a.m. to hike.

It was constant ups and downs between all the peaks. Keith fell and bloodied his arm.

We thought it was really dusty on the ridge only to realize it was pollen. It actually looked like green fog. That's when it hit me... I was suffering from pollen sickness. That's why I was struggling so much. You may say, "I've never heard of pollen sickness." Well, be quiet! It's my story, and I'm saying I had it.

We made it over to A and got great pics. You can look straight down about 800 feet to the Carter hut in the valley.

We met two mature ladies who were headed back to Wildcat D, as we were, but they had come up through the Carter Notch. Daaaaaang! Brave ladies! I don't mind being a chicken. You never hear of SAR rescuing chickens.

We stopped to eat and hydrate before heading back. Snacks are most important and, I might add, the fun part of hiking. That's why I try to stop every tenth of a mile to snack. My pals don't care to snack that much and are always complaining about my stops, not realizing that complaining is a telltale sign that they need a snack. After eating a protein bar, I took off like a rocket. Keith and Ian were amazed that a little food could heal pollen sickness, but it wasn't that at all. I was determined not to let those ladies pass us on the way back to the parking lot. I have some respectability. Not much, but some.

It was at this time, when I was moving quite quickly that I had a horrible fall. My hiking pole slid into a crevasse on a particularly steep section. I fell over and down some rocks, broke my hiking poles, cut a deep gash in my right hand and smashed my right shoulder. The other two guys were in shock after seeing my fall, knowing that there was a slim chance of survival. I bravely got up, hid the blood flow and said, "I'm OK. Let's keep moving." Here' another tip: if you fall and you're not hurt, but your companions are laughing, act hurt. They'll feel bad and it will shut them up. If you fall and are really hurt, suck it up and tell everyone you're fine.

It keeps your pals off guard and anyway, showing pain is not the way of mountain men.

I was concerned about how I was going to tell Darlene that the new poles she bought me for Christmas as a replacement for the old ones were now broken as well. Keith said that I should just ask her, "What is worse, being airlifted in a rescue or breaking a hiking pole?" I thought that was a brilliant idea. Just then, we heard voices closing in behind us. Those dang ladies! I put on the afterburners and we were out of there like a shot.

Up, down, up, down... equals a total of seven Wildcat peaks when you do an in and out.

We arrived back at D, and it was time for the miserable descent of two and a half miles down a ski slope. I became aware of a mistake I had made by not trimming my toenails. That leads to severe toe jamming and that leads to PAIN.

My knees were stiffening up to the point of no return, when we made it to the parking lot. It was a short ride to Dairy Queen. Darlene called while we were there and asked what I wanted for supper. I quickly blurted out, "Pizza and ice cream." The other guys stared in amazement, shaking their heads.

When I got home, I asked Darlene what she thought was worse: having to be air rescued or breaking a hiking pole? She was thinking for a moment, and I thought this could go either way, when she finally said, "Breaking a hiking pole." I gave her a kiss and told her I loved her and headed off to the shower. While drying off, I could hear her talking to a funeral director about the cost of a cemetery plot. I am not sure what that was all about, but I know she takes good care of me.

This hike really took it out of me, and I am seriously thinking about quitting. I only have four mountains left and the other guys are really encouraging me, but I just don't know if my knees and legs can do it. The remaining hikes are doozies.

Well, maybe just Owl's Head.

And maybe Mt. Madison.

And that, my friend, is hiking.

36 THE STORY OF
MT. ADAMS & MT. MADISON

These two mountains are now off my list, leaving me two peaks left to complete all forty-eight. I actually think I'm going to finish this thing. It is getting unbelievably exciting for a number of reasons. First, it is really a culmination of incredibly hard work with memorable stories and scars. Secondly, I will start saving money on gas. I think so far, I've consumed an amount equal to an Exxon oil tanker by driving the two hours to the Whites. Most non-hikers would never realize the whole experience of hiking. Certainly, the ride north is part of the overall experience. Oh, there is also the banter, teasing, haranguing, and abuse I put up with from my buddies that sets the tone for the whole day. Honestly, if I could learn to berate myself, I could easily take up solo hiking. Those guys are on me like an Apache on a Conestoga wagon. Women are not like that.

Women are always edifying and kind. You hear them say things like, "You got this," or "You go, girl." Guys, on the other hand, are always clowning and poking fun at each other. Just the other day I said to David, "You go girl." Hahaha!

Getting back to the drive up north, let's not forget the colonoscopy called Route 16. There is nothing that sucks the anticipation of getting to a hike like being stuck behind someone doing 45 in a 50. Everyone knows 50 really means 60.

Then, when heaven opens and a passing lane appears, the slow driver shoots up to 70. Ahhhhhh!!! But I don't swear, and I don't use childish hand signs, I simply cut them off and send them into the trees where their car explodes into flames and….. Ken, Ken, wake up. Sorry about that. Suffice it to say, if you drive Route 16, you understand completely.

Another sunny day appeared in the middle of one of the wettest springs in recorded history, so I contacted my old hiking buddy, Keith Tilton, and said, "I'm thinking of hiking Mt. Maddison." He said that he had to sleep in that day, and I hadn't even mentioned a day yet. After some pressure and the promise of $20, he was in. We looked at maps and did the normal research and decided to attack Adams and then jump over to Madison. Remember the old "I can do that" hikers' sickness? I had an extreme case of it.

I knew it would be a long day, so I picked Keith up at 4:30 a.m. It meant that I had to get up three hours earlier than usual, while the old feller only had to get up fifteen minutes earlier than usual.

We stopped off at Dunkin's and fueled up. America runs on Dunkin's. Our hike began at 7 a.m. up the Airline Trail. For some reason, I felt like I was dragging. I told Keith, "I'm going to take baby steps because I can't get the motor going." Truth be known, I think the motor was seized. Up, up and away! We passed a group of six hikers in their thirties and forties. Did you hear that? I'm now passing people. We passed another solo hiker. When we hit the tree line, I was now hydrating on Propel. I think it's made from rocket fuel extract. We passed a husband and wife with their daughter on the false summit that makes up the last ascent of Adams. Was I dreaming? Was I actually passing people?

This trail turned real tough real fast. I later found out it was on the 'Terrifying Twenty-five List'. In fact, I realized that I had done five of the 25. How did that happen? I tried to avoid that stuff like the kissing booth at a leper colony.

The wind on the last ascent was gusting at about 35 mph, so we stopped to layer up. I put on my windbreaker as fast as I could because parasailing off Adams didn't appeal to me just then. The views of the Carter Ridge and the other peaks in the Presidential Range were amazing. The sheer ruggedness of it all was exhilarating.

We got some great pics and videos at the summit and then headed over to the Madison hut. On the way, another hiker said, "You're in luck. They're still serving breakfast." At 11:30 a.m.? I popped inside to see a large bowl of cold oatmeal that looked like cement. As I tried to lift the spoon, it was stuck in the oatmeal which was stuck in the bowl, and the whole thing lifted off the table. I chose instead to eat one of my Cliff bars and a chocolate protein drink. Here is a huge lesson for you. Don't buy protein drinks at a dollar store. It came out in chunks. Disgusting! Spend the extra .25 cents and get the fresh stuff.

After a short rest, our legs had begun to solidify like the oatmeal, but we still had Madison to do. Mt. Madison is half a mile from the hut, pitched at a 45° angle that looks like the Egyptians blew up a pyramid, but it kept its shape. What a push! Again, we passed four young women. After some rock scrambles, we summited to the most breath-taking 360° view imaginable. It was so beautiful that I started whooping and screaming. Some other hikers may have thought that I was oxygen-deprived, but It was truly spectacular.

The wind gusts were crazy. When you feel the force of the wind on these mountains that rise above the tree line, you come to appreciate the extreme force of nature. We hung around a long time on the summit just drinking in the scenery.

All things come to an end, and it was time to go. A half-mile of "scary" down to the hut and then the Valley Way Trail back to the parking lot.

By this time Keith and I were depleted. You can always tell because you're no longer talking, your eyes feel sunken in, your mouth won't close, and you are tripping over the smallest things, because your legs just won't lift your feet anymore. At times like this, your mind is moving at a million miles an hour, but all you can say is, "Will this #%$&*%^ trail ever end?"

Here's a little something that I do when descending a trail. It is inevitable that you see hikers coming up. As I look into their haggard, fatigued, bloodshot eyes, knowing they are considering throwing in the towel, I always cheer them up by saying, "You're almost there, not much farther." Now I know they still have four miles of the most God-forsaken trail to go, but false hope is better than no hope at all. Keith says that I'm being mean. How can it be mean when I've been saying the same thing to myself for the last five miles?

We staggered back to the car, not caring what anybody thought of us at that point. We were dirty, sweaty, thirsty, smelly and downright exhausted.

I couldn't wait to get out of my hiking boots. Here's another tip; always bring sneakers to change into and get out of those dang hiking boots. You'll be glad you did. I've seen times where I've unlaced my boots, took them off, and they kept on right on walking with me not in them. That's a sight to see.

We headed to Dunkin's for water. Cool, clear, water.

Of course, the hike doesn't end even when you get home because you have to deal with transferring photos, unpacking, showering, posting stuff, and icing the knees. Then you get to look forward to going to sleep, only to find that when you close your eyes, your mind still sees rocks, lots of rocks. You blink and rub your eyes but there they are... rocks. It really is kind of psychotic.

And that, my friend, is hiking.

Ken taking the last steps to reach the peak of Adams

37 THE STORY OF MT. MOOSILAUKE

Moosilauke is Abenaki for "a bald place". This peak really looks like it belongs in the Scottish Highlands more than in the New Hampshire Whites. Usually, the 4,000 footers are either in forested peaks with no view or on rugged rocky summits. Mt. Moosilauke, on the other hand, is a large grass-covered area. It has been referred to as the gentle giant, but this gentle giant totally kicked my butt.

It had only been three days since my old hiking buddy, Keith Tilton, and I had hiked Adams and Madison. I was feeling a little overconfident and wanted to do another peak. Keith had not done Moosilauke, but I had. Seeing how Keith had done Mt. Galehead a second time just so I would not have to hike alone, I figured I would be a real pal and hike Moosilauke again with him. I had forgotten about this mountain because the mind has a phenomenon called repression. Traumatic memories disappear like magic, unfortunately this one came back in living color.

Moosilauke is 800 feet higher than Galehead, but I'm not going to mention that because what is 800 feet between friends? It is only another 800 feet straight up God-forsaken rock, but that's nothing.

The weather forecast looked promising, so we made the drive north.

After gearing up, we hit the Glencliff trail and were only a short distance in when we jumped a black bear. It was quickly moving away from us which is way better than moving towards us.

I tried to say, "Oh, Keith, look, a bear!" but in reality, I stood there with my mouth open and nothing intelligible would come out. I had the same exact experience when I had to give oral reports in school. Within seconds, the crashing sounds faded, and the bear had disappeared. That's more than I can say of what happened in my underwear.

People often wonder if we see wildlife on these hikes. The most common thing I see is the black fly that lands on the inside of my glasses and crosses my field of vision right as I'm trying to step on the right rock to prevent needing an airlift rescue. Other than that, there is the occasional toad or chipmunk. The bear was a sight to be seen... and repressed. Every image I have of bears comes straight from the movie *The Revenant*. You know the part when Leonardo DiCaprio gets torn to pieces by the grizzly. Why I watch that stuff is beyond me because that is what I think of every time I think of bears. I wish I could encounter more wildlife, but I think my gasping for breath while hiking drives them off into another State.

The trail became steeper as we went higher and I felt like I was not performing well; even so, we were making good time. (Also, it was 800 feet higher than Galehead.) I am always amazed at how steep and long these 4,000 footer trails are. They ain't easy, unless you're in shape that is.

I have begun drinking Propel drink mix in my hydration bladder, and the combination creates some kind of strange gas that leads to mild flatulence. As I am usually in the front, Keith isn't too happy about the whole deal. He was murmuring and making derogatory comments the whole hike. I did notice his handkerchief came out more often than normal. I really don't know the chemistry behind it, but within minutes of drinking from my hydration bladder, a pressure would build in my abdomen. It was kind of like the supervolcano underneath Yellowstone. Then there would be a mild release. Ok, maybe not so mild. Birds would fly from their nests screeching in terror and squirrels fell from trees limp and lifeless. The echo reverberated through the range like thunder. I would just act as if nothing happened, but Keith would start muttering something about SAR finding a murdered hiker someday.

Did I mention that Moosilauke is 800 feet higher than Galehead?

After reaching the ridge trail, we found it enjoyable. It was relatively flat with great views, a pleasant stroll as we made our way to the summit. At the top, we enjoyed a nice lunch and probably spent more time at this summit than any other because the views were spectacular, and it was cooler than the stifling 90° temps down in the flatlands. We took some great pics then headed out.

As we hiked down, I set a pace that was too fast. I don't know why I put myself through such a grueling descent, but I knew I would need to ice my knees again.

Maybe I was just trying to distance myself from Keith as he was looking for a large stick to throw at me. My goodness, the man was in the military. You'd think he'd have heard someone break wind before. Did I mention that Moosilauke is 800 feet higher than Galehead?

Keith and I are now tied for only needing two more peaks to finish the forty-eight.

Keith is a great friend who began this adventure with me a long time ago, and we are now within two peaks of finishing. It's getting real. Did I mention that Moosilauke is 800 feet higher than Galehead?

And that, my friend, is hiking.

Have you ever had an experience in life where you said, "Never again"? Examples that come to mind would be having your wisdom teeth extracted without Novocain or eating sushi at a Kansas truck stop or having a colonoscopy with a GoPro or for me... climbing Owl's Head.

38   THE STORY OF MT. OWL'S HEAD

I read in a write-up recently that most people attempting to complete the forty-eight 4,000 footers of New Hampshire push Owl's Head to the end of the list. Various reasons are suggested for this decision:

- It is a long 18-mile round trip from the Lincoln Woods Center into the middle of the Pemigewasset wilderness.

- It is only 4,025 feet and does not have a view.

- It has an unmaintained rockslide trail (the official trail going up to the summit)

- It includes hand over hand scrambles over the steep rock; arduous water crossings; the bugs are horrendous; and then there is the mud.

I say it is not any one of these in particular, but all of them rolled together times ten.

My good hiking buddy, Keith Tilton, and I had planned Owl's Head as one of our last. Not "the" last mind you, because you want to end on a mountain that is worth celebrating and this hump from hell is not celebratory.

My alarm clock started screaming at me at four in the morning saying that you've got to get up and hike Owl's Head. Keith, on the other hand, only had to get up a half-hour earlier than normal because he is an early riser. He is the guy that wakes up the roosters to let them know it is time to start their day. We got in the hiking car and headed to the great North to start our adventure.

Let me explain the hiking car. My wife had recently bought a new car, but we still had the old one, a 2006 Hyundai Sonata with 170,000 miles on it. It had some rust spots, but my repairs left it looking worse than the rust. I have a truck that doesn't get great gas mileage, so I kept the car and had written "Hike NH 48" with a black Sharpie across the back bumper. The hiking car had gone on over 40 hikes with us. Every excursion north had me wide-eyed, driving the hiking car in the morning darkness, while my hiking companions slept like babies. They got the extra rest that put me behind the eight ball and made me a little more sluggish.

I am told Owl's Head derives its name from the part of its summit that resembles an owl's head. I believe if you look at it at just the right angle, at just the right time of day, in the right season, with just the right amount of LSD, it looks like an owl.

Seriously, folks, I see nothing here that represents an owl other than the fact that owls eat their prey whole and later poop out the fur and bones, which is exactly the way I felt after this hike, like I had been eaten and pooped out.

Keith and I headed off and made pretty good time overall averaging a speed of two miles per hour. We came to our first water crossing, and I took my boots and socks off, while Keith went upstream to look for a crossing. I crossed and waited about 30 minutes for him to show up. He decided to take his boots and socks off about a quarter-mile upstream and cross there. I don't know why he went that far looking for a rock crossing, but he did. At the second water crossing, we were both in agreement to remove our boots and socks. As I waded across, I slipped on a rock and experienced a full Jacques Cousteau underwater adventure. Gosh, hiking is fun! I was now soaking wet.

We made it to the base of the mountain and met a young couple who had camped out and were finishing up a multiple peak adventure with Owl's Head. (The man had previously completed the Appalachian Trail.) As he started up the slide, he stopped to get pictures of how steep it was. When an experienced AT hiker stops to get a picture of the steepness of a trail, this unexperienced hiker knew I was in for a real roller coaster ride.

It seems that each mountain hiked prepares you for the next one. All my previous mountain experiences culminated into this one event. I am going up the steepest trail I have ever experienced, the whole time wondering how I will ever survive the descent.

I don't know what was worse, the adrenaline from the steepness of the slide trail or the panic arising from imagining the trip down.

When we arrived at the top, we knew that it was a false summit, and most people miss traveling the .2 miles to the actual peak. We did the dance to the real summit, which included going under blowdowns on all fours only to find a cairn of about 20 stones. It was pathetic. Someone needs to put something up there to make that trip worthwhile. A Dairy Queen would be perfect.

When we started down, I had heard of the Brutus bushwhack that bypassed the slide trail. I accidentally took it and within a short distance we found ourselves off trail on the side of a very steep mountain, blindly bushwhacking our way down. I stepped on some rocks on a steep section, and they popped out, and I went for a tumble. As Keith relates, it's a good thing I was stopped by hitting my head on that tree or I would still be rolling down that mountain.

It was a scary thought to imagine what would have happened if I had gotten hurt eight miles out in the middle of nowhere, off-trail, somewhere on the side of a very steep mountain, with no cell reception. I'm pretty sure Keith would have hiked out and not told anyone, because he was still mad about the mild flatulence on Moosilauke.

Keith took the lead, and his internal GPS system soon connected us to the defined bushwhacking trail. We hit the main trail at the bottom and headed out with our new friends joining us. Some people have an uncanny sense of direction and then there's me. Darlene gets scared even when I tell her I'm going to get the mail.

We took the Blackwater Pond bushwhack, bypassing the river crossings on the way out and saving me from taking another swim.

It seemed like it took forever to get back to the Lincoln Woods Trail and, even though it's the trail that never ends, we knew we were within a few miles of the car.

When we got to the parking lot, we were covered in mud, scratched up, dehydrated, and just plum worn out. I had brought a jug of lemonade with ice and left it in the car; it was the best tasting drink ever.

On our way home, just north of Concord, the infamous hiking car blew its engine and gave up the ghost. The tow truck came. I cried. Keith hummed 'Amazing Grace'. Darlene came to the rescue to bring Keith and me home. We loaded everything from one car into the other. When Keith and I got into the car, Darlene immediately put down all four windows, at the same time exclaiming, "Bug spray would smell better than you guys right now." Keith and I didn't know what she was referring to. We were just glad to be heading home.

I will say that even when we had four guys in the hiking car after a ten-miler, we never smelled anything.

Owl's Head was number 47. And I will say, "Never again!!!"

And that, my friend, is hiking.

Farewell to the hiking car.

39 THE STORY OF MT. JEFFERSON, SWEET #48

This was going to be the first hike in a long time where Keith, Ian, David and I would be together again. Our goal was to summit Jefferson, which would finish the forty-eight for Keith and me, and then go over to Mt. Washington because Ian needed both peaks. David had finished his forty-eighth the week before on Mount Isolation because he was determined that Keith and I would not pass him.

I guess he was afraid that if we finished before him, we would never let him live it down. My goodness! That would never have crossed my mind. Keith on the other hand…?

As it turned out, Ian had come down with a summer cold and was unable to go. In hindsight, it worked out better because I don't know if I would have had the strength to make it up to Washington.

As I look back over the last couple of years, Ian has become a great friend and a really good hiker. I knew him as a kid and we lost touch for years. He had contacted me after seeing my Facebook posts and wanted to go on a hike. One hike later he was bitten by the disease and was on his way to complete the forty-eight. He is an awesome young man with a great sense of humor. I really enjoyed doing the Belknap Red Line patch with Ian, and I look forward to hiking with him more in the future.

David, Keith, and I had decided to do the Caps Ridge Trail to Mt. Jefferson. The weather was picture perfect. A nice cool start to what would turn out to be a very hot day. As we started our ascent, I was in the lead and making pretty good time. Then we began to hit the Caps. The first one was fun and very interesting with the holes drilled in the rock by ancient waterfalls as the glaciers melted. The next two Caps, however, were up incredibly steep cliffs. This time our pictures captured the difficulty of this climb. I don't know if it was the strenuous constant uphill or the emotional and adrenaline rushes that sapped my strength, but I noticed I was beginning to fade. Keith, on the other hand, hit those cliffs like a monkey. I was amazed because I know he doesn't like heights, but he told me later that he just decided to never look down and look at the next rock that was above him and pushed on. Keith is in amazing shape for a 70-year-old. He has become a good friend and has been my faithful companion since the very first mountain all the way through to the end of the forty-eight. Not to mention that he and I did all the Castle in the Cloud and Belknap Range Trails, as well as some of the 'Fifty-two with a View'. He has listened to my constant complaining and whining through the heat, bugs, freezing cold, falls, and pretty much everything about hiking and still hung in there with me. Now, that's a pal.

As we hiked higher up the Caps, I was amazed at the difficulty. Later I discovered the trail is on the 'Terrifying Twenty-Five List'. I now realize there is a market for REI to sell hiking diapers.

Reaching the summit of Jefferson, I stepped on a round rock; it rolled just enough for me to take a tumble and smash my bad knee again. My first thought was of a helicopter lifting me off the peak. What a way to not finish, because the rules say you must ascend and descend on your own power. At first, there was no problem but later it would start stiffening up and give me some real problems.

Dave, Ken & Keith on top of Mt. Jefferson – last of the 48!

We were amazed there was no sign marking the summit. Also, the flies were incredible. What were flies doing on top of a 5,700 foot mountain? They were sure as heck not going to get any of my Italian sandwich. As I sat there eating and reflecting on our hike, fear began to set in about going down those cliffs. I don't mind being labeled a chicken. I kind of like chickens. I just did not like the idea of those Caps. So, I pulled the plug and told my buddies I was going down another route. Keith and I decided to skirt Mt. Clay and pick up the Jewel Trail descending from Mount Washington. David, on the other hand, was going to go down the Caps Ridge Trail, get Keith's truck, and meet us in the parking lot. David is an amazing athlete. He is in terrific physical shape and could give any goat a run for its money on those cliffs. Keith and I were not crazy about having to split up with him, but we knew if anyone could handle solo hiking, it was David. He is another that has become a good friend over the years, and this was now the third time he had to bail my bacon out of the fire. He always did it with a smile and never complained, even though this time, he had to wait two hours in the truck for us to return.

Here's another hiking tip: find the right companions and your hiking experiences will be more enjoyable than you could ever imagine. I hiked with the best. If you have a hard time finding the right folks to hike with, do what I did. Go to the State Mental Hospital and pick them out like puppies at an SPCA.

The trail over to Mt. Clay and then on to the Jewell Trail was slow going because of all the uneven rocks up there. It would be so easy to twist or sprain an ankle that I am amazed there are not more injuries on these peaks. I hiked a 9,000 footer in California when I was visiting my son. It was nothing like the Whites, but as it was CA, the trail was groomed and had safe spaces in case your feelings got hurt.

The farther Keith and I descended, the more my knees started stiffening up, and my feet became really sore. Situation normal! I was eating Advil like M&Ms.

As we got within a mile from the trailhead, we met a dad who had lost two 11-year-olds. They had gotten out ahead of him and yet were not at the parking lot. You could see the concern on his face. We offered to help and told him we would say a prayer for him. You just cannot separate from kids in these mountains. I know how hard it is because, years ago, my two kids pulled away from me on Mt. Lafayette.

After reaching the parking lot, I was done in. The heat and the humidity had pulled everything out of me. I was sweating like a dog. I was feeling pain in every part of my body and never wanted to return to any of these mountains again.

I felt a bittersweet emotion at completing the forty-eight. I never thought I would do it in my condition, yet here I was at the last mountain. It had been the most rewarding challenge of my life but now it was over.

That night I iced my knees and took some more Advil. To my surprise, the next morning, I awoke feeling amazingly well. So well that I texted Ian and told him to let me know when he was going to do Mt. Zealand and I would go with him.

The sickness continues. I'm thinking of buying a new book that's out: *New Hampshire's 52 with a View: A Hiker's Guide* by Ken MacGray.

40 CANNON MOUNTAIN, PART 2

"My patches came in! My patches came in!" That was the cry that resounded through our home when the patch for completing the forty-eight 4,000 footers arrived. When I got the patches, I cried like a new mom. For me, that patch was a badge of honor that said I had accomplished something very few people have done. I ordered more patches and started sewing them on everything I owned. Darlene drew the line on underwear as she said no one would see them there and no one would want to. I also ordered a hat with a patch on it and some cool tee shirts.

Then it happened.

Ian texted me and asked if I wanted to hike Cannon with him.

Officially, I was done! Retired! Finished!

But something had happened. I had recently been thinking about hiking constantly. I daydreamed about it. I night dreamed about it. I would catch myself looking at my maps and pictures of past hikes… It had happened. The disease had taken over. I had even started the 'Fifty-two with a View' list.

This from the guy who whined, cried, and complained his way up every single trail.

In a weakened moment of poor judgment, I saw myself texting Ian back saying, "I'd love to hike Cannon."

I quickly justified my actions by reminding myself that it had been 20 years since I had last hiked Cannon, and if I did it again, I would be able to include one last chapter in this book.

My temporary cloud of denial was soon to vanish in the sunlight of sheer fear.

Allow me to share.

After texting Ian, I immediately contacted my good hiking buddy, Keith, who had previously hiked Cannon and taken a nasty fall on it. Of course, he started with the usual excuses of Legionaries disease and smallpox but reluctantly caved in and said he would go.

We rallied at EMS in Concord and headed north. After arriving at the Lafayette campground parking area, we geared up and headed out. The peaks in Franconia Notch were frost-covered and looked amazing.

We took the Lonesome Lake Trail to the lake then a nice flat walk over planks to a steep section of the trail followed by another flat walk to the Kinsman Ridge Trail. The temperature was hovering at 30° and we started to encounter the frost, especially on the tree roots. By this time both Ian and Keith had fallen twice. I was fortunate. And a little more coordinated. We headed up the trail like lemmings rushing off a cliff. Once again, I was in the lead. The next thing I knew, I was rock climbing a length of trail that was so steep I was shaking like Jell-O in an earthquake.

There was a moment or two of second-guessing the wisdom of hiking such a steep trail with a hint of frost on it. Even though all three of us said that if we were alone, we would have turned back, the challenge of not being the one to let the others down caused me to push on. I was now sweating like a sumo wrestler in a sauna. We came to what appeared to be a recent rockslide that had demolished enough of the trail that people had started bushwhacking a new trail around it.

Keith started praying, Ian was crying, and I had lost the function of speech as well as other bodily controls. It was crazy steep!

Sheer grit and determination got us past this nightmare of a trail. As we leveled off and headed to the summit, we met two young women who were starting to head down the trail. When I warned them of the dangers, one looked at me as if to say, "Are we wearing the same color panties?" Dang, these women hikers are tough!

We were socked in with clouds and the summit looked like Antarctica. Rime ice covered everything. It was simply breathtaking. Thankfully we were prepared and dressed for the occasion but with the windchill and being soaked from sweat we decided to head down. Between Ian's teeth chattering and Keith's knees knocking, it sounded like Blue Man Group on steroids.

When we got to the steeps Ian took the lead and started doing a butt-slide kind of crab walk descent. I must admit he was making good time, albeit looking a little mechanical. It is amazing what a little fear can do. Keith and Ian decided to take the newly formed bushwhack to avoid the cliff while I descended down the regular trail informing them that it was not too bad. Then the trail turned and leveled off where the rockslide had occurred, and I found myself having to cross twelve feet of steeply angled rock with boulders on my left and a 15 foot drop-off on my right. Oh ya, it was THAT bad! I froze. My mind was calculating scenarios faster than a math whiz on crack. None of them ended well. Ian said, "I'm not watching this," as he crabbed down the trail. Keith pulled out his phone, muttering what sounded like, "This will make the evening news."

I put my left foot out first and brought it back, then my right. Realizing it looked like I was doing the Hokey Pokey, I began to cross. I can't remember if I walked or if I was shaking so bad that I vibrated across, but I do know that the last few steps were hurried. When I realized that I had survived the foolish stunt, I talked Keith into taking photos of the recreated suspenseful scene. Stories belong to the survivors; doctor bills to the rest.

By the time we reached Lonesome Lake, a lot of hikers were coming up the trail. I don't know why, but I started asking them, "You going to Cannon?" Most of them said, "No, just to the lake." Ian started busting on me on why I was asking everyone that question. Maybe my head had swelled a little. I had just accomplished an amazing feat that the other two avoided. Then one hiker saw my tee shirt and asked, "Have you hiked all forty-eight?" I proudly replied that I had and that I just finished Cannon for the "second" time, prompting Keith to ask me later if I needed another backpack for my ego. Sheeesh. Can't a guy feel a little pride in cheating death twice on the same mountain?

I mean, it is hard to be proud of your mountain accomplishments when you have to go home and change your underwear!

On the way home we had lots of laughs and high-spirited conversation, most of which centered around them not wanting to hike with me anymore. What great friends. Can't wait to hike with them again.

And that, my friend, is the disease known as hiking the forty-eight.

41 FRIENDS

I know I have poked some fun at my hiking buddies, but honestly, they are the best!

Keith, Ian, and David are great friends and we continue to hike together to this day. They have been a constant source of encouragement to me as I attempted to finish the forty-eight. I am now starting to knock off the 'Fifty-two with a View'. Bret, Tim, Dianna, Holly, Sue, and others I've hiked with are all top drawer folks. I can never say enough good about all of them because I'm trying to cover myself from possible lawsuits.

In all fairness, I made an offer for my hiking buddies to turn in a one-page report on what it was like hiking with me. David and Keith couldn't do it, because every time they started to write the paper got wet from tears of admiration. Ian was the only one to submit something. As promised, I corrected grammar but not content. I did add at the end what I believe David and Keith would have said if they could have kept it together.

Ian: I started hiking with PK (Pastor Ken) last July 2018. This would be my second 4,000 footer, the first one being over two years earlier. I had been seeing his posts of his hiking tales on social media for a while and told him I would love to accompany him on one of his hikes! I finally received a call that they were heading up to do Mt. Moriah and I went for it. I had been working on my conditioning and was ready for the challenge. The night before the hike, I decided to wear my sandals… the next morning I wised up figuring that wasn't a good idea. As we hiked up, PK didn't complain at all, and by not complaining at all, I mean he complained constantly. He complained about the slab rock, about the steepness… Sounded like he wanted to be home eating some Louie's Pizza on the couch watching his all-time favorite *Jeremiah Johnson*. But it was a successful hike. This was number two for me on a journey I never expected I would be on. It would change my life.

Fast forward to our first overnight on the Bonds. It was a terribly hot day above tree line, the sun pounding on us all the time we did Bond Cliff, Bond, and West Bond and back over to Bond Cliff to go out the way we had gone in. Everyone was tuckered out! This is the point where PK is going to say we left him and his buddy, Keith. But this is really where PK passed out, and we had to heroically carry him off the mountain. Just kidding!

He doesn't give himself enough credit. For instance, you'll read his story about Wildcats where we charged up the Polecat trail at about two and a half miles an hour and he was wondering why he wasn't feeling 100% at the top. We talked him into continuing over to the second peak. He ate some Beef Jerky that expired I think sometime around the time he was born. He then RACED back to the Polecat trail so fast you would think he was being chased by the bears that make him afraid to venture out with us on overnight hikes.

Thanks for all the great hikes, PK! Looking forward to more!

*Although these are not their words exactly, I'm pretty sure Dave &
Keith would say something along these lines:*

David: PK is the ruggedest hiker I've ever seen. He's not afraid
of any trail, no matter how steep. His knowledge of all things hiking
is amazing. I feel safer hiking with someone like him. He is also one
of the most fashionable hikers I've ever seen. It's like every time he
hikes, he makes a new fashion statement.

Keith: I'm honored to have PK ask me to accompany him on
hiking the forty-eight. I never dreamed this was something a guy
my age could ever accomplish, but his constant encouragement
allowed me to do it. He is the most optimistic and positive guy I
know. While driving with him, I have learned to become a
respectful and courteous driver. I'm glad to call him my friend.

Closing Thoughts:

I hope after reading this book you've had lots of laughs and, if you're a hiker, you saw yourself in some of my struggles. If you are not a hiker, but considering it, I hope you rise to the challenge knowing that if I can do it, you can too. I also hope you have the satisfaction of knowing the profits from this book will go to supporting NH SAR. These men and women do an amazing job responding in all kinds of weather and have never been busier than they are now with the growing popularity of hiking the NH 48.

Allow me to sign off with this simple truth I have learned in my life: God is the greatest mountain and Jesus is the trail.

Be blessed and hike safely!

ABOUT THE AUTHOR

Ken and his wife Darlene reside in Raymond, NH, where he has been a pastor for 30 years. They have a son, daughter & son-in-law as well as a grandson - who has yet to be introduced to hiking.

Ken is the Chaplain at the Raymond Police Department. He is also a PCC Level Life Coach with the International Coaching Federation. He has coached individuals, couples and workplace teams, helping them to achieve their goals in life.

He enjoys playing guitar, shooting, kayaking with Darlene, building wooden model ships, and writing.

Ken still suffers from the hiking addiction.

Made in the USA
Monee, IL
07 February 2020